D0590900

THE SCIENTIFIC LIVING SERIES
THE HOW AND WHY SCIENCE BOOKS

THE HOW AND WHY CLUB

George Willard Frasier
Helen Dolman MacCracken
Donald G. Decker
Daniel C. McNaughton
Illustrated by
Guy Brown Wiser
Claude E. Leet

THE L. W. SINGER COMPANY

Syracuse, *New York*

THE HOW AND WHY CLUB

Printed in the U.S.A.

81225.0

A Visit to the Airport

Jimmy, Bob, Nancy, and Jane were on their way to the airport. They were riding their bicycles. They were on their way to meet their new teacher, Mr. Thorne. He was to arrive at the airport in his own airplane.

"We must be careful where we ride," said Jimmy. "There are a great many automobiles on the streets this morning." So the children rode with care. They watched the traffic at the corners. They made signals with their hands before they turned corners. They used the same signals that automobile drivers use in the streets. They held their left hands straight out before turning left. They held their left hands straight up before turning right. When they arrived at the airport they put their bicycles in the rack provided for bicycles. Only careless boys and girls leave their bicycles on the ground where someone might fall over them.

Of course the children were excited. Mr. Thorne was their first man teacher. He owned and piloted his own airplane. The paper said Mr. Thorne would arrive about ten. A long time before ten the children were waiting at the airport.

Jimmy knew a great deal about the airport because his father was the manager. Jimmy had been there many times with his father. Jimmy asked his father to tell the children about the airport.

"Our most important job," said Jimmy's father, "is to enforce all safety regulations. No pilot is allowed to land his plane at the airport unless he has permission from the towerman." Jimmy's father pointed to the glassed-in tower above the main building. The children could see the towerman busily engaged in talking over a radio.

"When an airplane approaches the airport and the pilot wishes to land, he must get permission from the towerman," said Jimmy's father. "If the plane has a radio, the pilot calls the towerman and gets his instructions for landing. If he does not have a radio, the instructions are given with a light gun. If the towerman shoots a green light toward the plane, the pilot knows that everything is clear for landing. A red light tells him that it is not safe to land. Then the pilot must circle around until he gets the green light. If the towerman did not control all airplanes, there would be no safety at the airport."

Suddenly the children saw an airplane approaching the airport. "I wonder if that is Mr. Thorne's plane," said Jane.

"No," said Jimmy's father, "that is the nine-fifty passenger plane from Chicago. It is much larger than a private plane. It has two engines. Most private planes have only one."

"Did the pilot of the passenger plane have permission to land?" asked Nancy.

"Yes," said Jimmy, "all passenger planes have radios. The towerman has been talking to the pilot for some time. The towerman has told him the direction and strength of the wind. He has also told him which runway to use."

The big plane came down to earth. It landed on one of the paved runways. The plane then taxied to the gate before the main building. Some steps were wheeled up to the door. The door opened. The passengers came out.

While the plane was landing no one was allowed outside the gate. The runways were clear. In fact, everything was done to insure the safety of the plane and passengers.

"Oh, here he comes," cried Bob. In the excitement about the passenger plane they had forgotten to watch for Mr. Thorne. Sure enough a small plane was approaching the airport. Then the towerman gave it the green light. Soon the little plane had made a landing. It taxied up to the gate. The children greeted Mr. Thorne.

"We are glad you arrived safely," said Nancy. "We were worried about you."

"There is little need to worry about anyone who flies a plane or rides in one," said Mr. Thorne. "There are many safety regulations and all pilots must obey them."

"What happens when a pilot does not obey the regulations?" asked Bob.

"He is grounded," said Mr. Thorne, "and is not allowed to fly a plane."

Mr. Thorne thanked the children for meeting him. He told them he must get a space in the hangar for his plane. He also wanted to get the engine checked. So the children rode back home on their bicycles. Each one was anxious to learn more about Mr. Thorne's airplane.

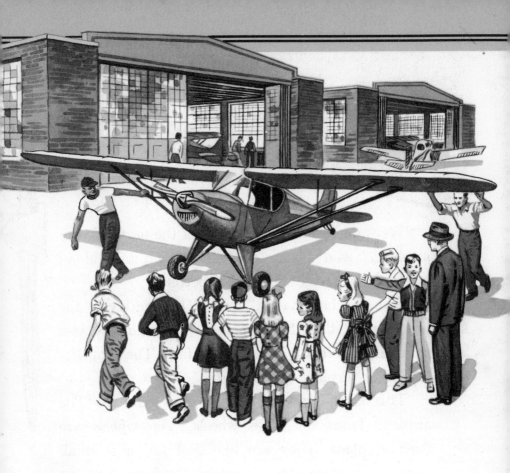

Mr. Thorne's Airplane

Jimmy told the children about Mr. Thorne's airplane. All the children were anxious to see it. So Mr. Thorne took all the children in his room to the airport to see his plane.

The children watched with excitement while the little plane was being wheeled out of the hangar. Everyone had questions to ask.

"We want to know the names of the parts of your airplane," said Nancy. "Then we can talk about airplanes and read about them better."

"I know what that is," said Bob, pointing to the propeller. "It is the propeller. The engine rotates it rapidly. In fact it spins it very fast. The propeller makes the airplane go forward."

"This is the landing gear," said Jimmy. "The airplane lands on these wheels. The wheels are fixed in place. They are like that on most small planes. On large planes used by the army and the air lines, the wheels are folded up out of the way after the plane takes off. They are put down again when the airplane is about to land."

"The body of the plane is called the *fuselage*," said Mr. Thorne. "See how the wing is fastened to the fuselage. This airplane has only one wing. It is called a *monoplane*. Planes with two wings, one above the other, are called *biplanes*."

"What are these flap-like things on the edge of the wing?" asked Jane.

"Those are *ailerons*," said Mr. Thorne. "The pilot moves them up and down by moving the stick to the right and left. Watch, I'll show you." Mr. Thorne got into the pilot's seat. He showed the children the stick. Then he moved it. The children watched the ailerons move up and down.

"When one aileron goes up the other one goes down," cried Nancy. "They work just opposite to each other."

"That is right," said Mr. Thorne. "They are used to lower or raise the wing in turning the plane."

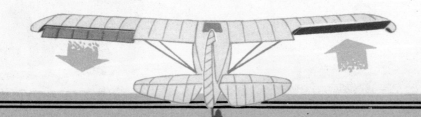

"This flap-like thing on the tail is called the *elevator*," said Mr. Thorne. "The pilot can move it up and down. When the elevator goes down the tail goes up and the nose goes down. When the elevator goes up the tail goes down and the nose of the plane goes up. So the elevator helps the pilot bring his plane down or take it up higher."

"This is the *rudder*," said Mr. Thorne. "It is like the elevator only it stands straight up. The pilot can move it to the right or left. It is used to turn the nose of the plane to the right or left."

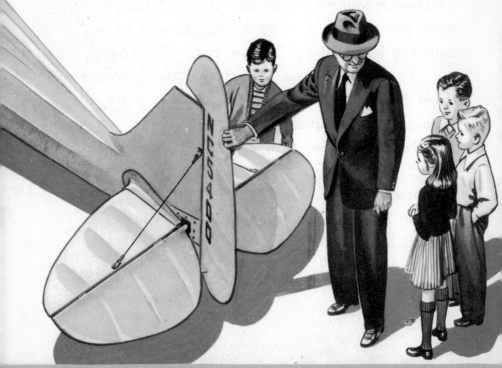

"There are a great many other names to learn," said Mr. Thorne, "but we will learn them later. We will make a list of these new words in the science class tomorrow."

The next morning the children were together again in their science class. Mr. Thorne had drawn two diagrams on the blackboard.

"Would you like to put the new words we learned yesterday on the blackboard?" said Mr. Thorne. All the children wanted to help, so they selected Nancy to write the words. She wrote the new words on the blackboard as the children gave them to her. Here is Nancy's list.

WING   FUSELAGE

NOSE   AILERON

TAIL   STICK

PROPELLER   ELEVATOR

LANDING GEAR   RUDDER

Then Jimmy put each new word on Mr. Thorne's diagrams. Can you do it?

"I think science is fun," said Jane. "We studied science last year. I wish we could study science again this year."

"You may study science every day if you wish to," said Mr. Thorne. "What would you like to study?"

"I would like to study about all kinds of things the way scientists do," said Bob.

"What are scientists?" asked Nancy.

"I know," said Jimmy. "Scientists are men who study and experiment to find out things. Is that right, Mr. Thorne?"

"Yes, that's a good answer," said Mr. Thorne.

"I should like to be a scientist some day," said Jimmy.

"That would be fine, Jimmy," said Mr. Thorne. "How shall we study science this year?" he asked the children.

"We can do experiments," said Bob. "Last year we did many experiments. They were lots of fun."

"We can go on field trips and look for things," said Nancy. "Last year we went on field trips. We learned many things."

"Let's have a science club!" said Jimmy.

"That would be fun," said Nancy.

"That's a good idea," said Mr. Thorne. "You may have a meeting every morning if you like."

So the children formed a science club. They named it the How and Why Club. Jimmy was elected president. Nancy was made secretary. Mr. Thorne was made a member of the club. The club met every morning at nine o'clock.

The next morning at nine o'clock Jimmy called the How and Why Club to order.

"If we are to study science," said Jimmy, "we must learn how scientists work."

"We must have some problems to work on," said Dick. "Where can we find problems?"

"That is easy," said Jimmy. "We will think of questions that we want answered."

So the children went to work. Here are some of the questions they wanted answered.

1. What makes an airplane stay in the air?
2. How does electricity work?
3. How does a compass work?
4. Why are the stars in different places at different times of the year?
5. Why don't the sun and the moon come up at the same time each day?
6. What makes plants grow?
7. How can fish live in water when we can't?
8. How does a spider make a web?
9. What does the body do with food?
10. Why should we eat vegetables?
11. Why does mother keep milk in the refrigerator?
12. What makes food spoil?
13. What causes measles and mumps?
14. How many different kinds of trees are in our school yard? How can we tell them apart?

"That's a fine list of questions," said Mr. Thorne. "We will answer many of them in our How and Why Club."

"How will we find the answers?" asked Susan.

"We can experiment," said Jimmy. "That's the way to find some answers."

"We can ask people who know about science," said Dick. "I know my dad can help us name the trees in the school yard."

"We can read," said Bob. "We can find some answers in books."

"We can ask Mr. Thorne about some of them," said Jimmy. "I'm sure he will help us."

"We can take field trips and observe some things," said Jane.

"Those are all good suggestions," said Mr. Thorne. "If you are to study science, you must do experiments carefully. You must make accurate observations on field trips. You must make careful reports. You must not guess at answers."

The meeting adjourned at nine-thirty.

A Trip to Andy Baker's Cellar

"Look at this big apple," said Bob at the next meeting of the science club. "My father bought two bushels of apples. We will have apples for a long time."

"My uncle sent us two boxes of oranges," said Dick. "We keep them in a cool part of the cellar. They will last until Christmas."

"My father has been putting potatoes and onions and cabbages in our cellar," said Bob. "He says they will keep until spring."

"My mother bought some baskets of peaches and grapes," said Nancy. "She cooked them right away and put them into glass jars. They are all stored in our cellar. We can have peaches or grape juice any time we want them next winter."

"I know a man who has vegetables for sale," said Jimmy. "He sells vegetables all winter. His name is Andy Baker. He has a vegetable cellar."

"I'd like to see his cellar," said Jane.

"I move that the How and Why Club take a trip to Andy Baker's vegetable cellar," said Dick.

"I second the motion," said Mr. Thorne.

The motion was carried.

The next morning the How and Why Club met at nine o'clock at Andy Baker's vegetable cellar.

The children were interested in the cellar. All they could see from the outside was the long pointed roof that was covered with a thick layer of straw and soil. The rest of the cellar was below the surface of the ground.

"Why is the roof covered with dirt?" asked Jane.

"Dirt protects the cellar from the heat of the sun in summer and from the cold air in winter," said Mr. Thorne. "By having the roof covered with dirt, Mr. Baker is able to keep his cellar at almost the same temperature all year round."

"He must have a furnace that he uses in winter," said Dick. "See those three chimneys on the roof."

"They don't look like regular chimneys," said Jimmy. "They are made of wood. They aren't used for a furnace, are they, Mr. Thorne?"

"No," said Mr. Thorne. "Those chimneys are there to allow fresh air to enter the cellar."

A driveway wide enough for an automobile went right into the cellar. The children walked down the driveway, through the big wide doors, and into the dark cellar. It was cool and dry inside.

The children found great quantities of vegetables in the cellar. There were piles of cabbages and baskets of lettuce and spinach. There were carrots, beets, turnips, white potatoes and some sweet potatoes, as well as bags of onions and crates of celery.

"You have a lot of food stored here, Mr. Baker," said Bob. "Will you sell all of it?"

"Most of it," said Andy. "But some of it I will keep to feed my rabbits and chickens. And some of it you're going to take back to school with you. How would you like that?"

The children's eyes shone. They watched Andy as he set out different piles of vegetables.

In the first pile he put a head of cabbage, a head of lettuce, and some spinach.

In the second pile he put a carrot, a beet, a turnip, and a big sweet potato.

In the third pile he put some kernels of corn, some beans, and a handful of nuts that he brought from his house.

Then he put a bunch of celery and a white potato in another place.

"Now I'm going to ask you a question," said Andy. "Why did I put these things in four piles?"

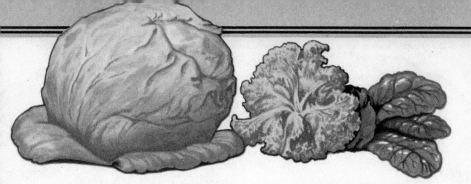

"I know why you put the spinach and lettuce with the cabbage," said Jimmy. "They are all leaves."

"I know why the carrot, beet, turnip, and sweet potato go together," said Jane. "They are all roots."

"Corn and beans and nuts are seeds," said Susan.

"Why are the celery and the white potato in another place?" asked Bob. "The potato looks like a root."

"The celery and the white potato are different from these other vegetables," said Mr. Thorne.

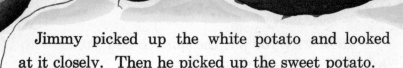

Jimmy picked up the white potato and looked at it closely. Then he picked up the sweet potato.

"Look!" he said. "The white potato doesn't look like a root. It doesn't come down to a point. The white potato has eyes on it. There are no eyes on the sweet potato."

"Those are good observations," said Mr. Thorne. "The white potato is not a root. It is a stem. Those eyes that you see, Jimmy, are buds."

"A stem!" cried Dick. "A potato grows under the ground. I thought stems grew above ground."

"Most of them do," said Mr. Thorne. "A tree trunk is a stem that grows above ground. Asparagus stems grow above ground. But a potato is an enlarged stem that grows under the ground."

"What is celery?" asked Bob.

"A bunch of celery is a bunch of leaves," said Mr. Thorne. "But celery is different from cabbage and lettuce and spinach. We eat the leaves of those vegetables. The part of celery that we eat is the enlarged leaf stalk."

"Here is an onion," said Nancy. "Where does it belong?"

"It doesn't look like a leaf," said Jane. "It doesn't look like a root, either."

"It isn't a seed," said Bob.

"I know," said Jimmy. "It's a bulb. It's like the narcissus bulbs we planted last year."

"When we cut a narcissus bulb in two, we saw a short stem with thick leaves around it," said Susan.

"We have been noticing how all these plants are different," said Mr. Thorne. "Can you tell how they are alike?"

"They all have food stored in them," said Jane.

"Cabbage and spinach and lettuce have food stored in their leaves," said Dick. "Carrots and beets and sweet potatoes have food stored in their roots."

"Beans and corn and nuts are seeds that have food stored in them," said Susan.

"The white potato has food stored in an enlarged underground stem," said Jane. "Celery and onions have stored food in them, too."

"Is the same kind of food stored in all of these plants?" asked Bob.

"No," said Mr. Thorne. "Not all plants store

the same kind of food. Some plants store one kind
of food; other plants store other kinds of food.

"Starch and sugar and fat are the most common
of the stored foods," he continued. "When we eat
plants, or anything made from plants, we eat the food
that has been stored to help the plants grow. For
example, corn stores starch. Cornstarch is made
from corn. When we eat a dish of cornstarch pudding
we eat starch, a food that is stored in corn. If
we put sugar on the pudding, we eat another kind of
food stored in plants. And if we put cream on it,
we eat fat, too."

"But cream doesn't come directly from plants,"
said Jimmy.

"Good for you, Jimmy," said Mr. Thorne. "Cream
doesn't come directly from plants. But the fat in
cream and butter is the same kind of food that some
plants store."

"Couldn't we do some experiments to learn for
ourselves about the food stored in plants?" asked
Jimmy.

"That's a good idea," said Dick. "We'll start our
experiments in tomorrow's club meeting."

The children thanked Mr. Baker and said good-bye
to him. Then they started back to school.

The First Experiments

Nancy's Experiment

"May I test some things for fat?" asked Nancy.

"Yes, indeed," said Mr. Thorne. "It would be a good idea to test first something you know has fat in it."

"Butter has fat in it," said Nancy. "So has fat meat." The next day she brought some butter and some suet to school.

"How can I test them?" she asked Mr. Thorne.

"You can use a clean piece of blotting paper," he told her. "Or you can use plain brown paper."

Nancy wasn't sure just how blotting paper would help test for fat, but she put a piece on the table. Then she put some butter on the paper. When she held the paper to the light, the children could see a round grease spot.

Next she tried the suet. She pressed it on the paper. That also made a grease spot on the paper.

"Fat makes a grease spot on blotting paper," said Nancy.

"Try some celery," said Susan. "Mr. Thorne said that some plants store the same kind of food that is in butter."

When Nancy cut a piece of celery and pressed it on the blotting paper, it made a wet spot instead of a grease spot. "Celery does not make the same kind of spot on blotting paper that fat does," said Nancy. "It must be that celery does not contain fat."

Then she tried some carrot and some white potato, but neither one made a grease spot on the paper.

"Try some nuts," suggested Dick.

When Nancy crushed a peanut on the blotting paper, it made a grease spot where it had been crushed.

Dick laughed. "That's the way paper looks when peanut butter gets on it. It must be because peanuts have fat in them."

Next Nancy crushed a walnut on the paper. It made a grease spot on the paper also. "Walnuts have fat in them," said Nancy.

Jimmy's Experiment

"I'd like to test some plants for starch," said Jimmy.

"That will be an interesting experiment," said Mr. Thorne. "Iodine will help you test starch in plants."

The next day Jimmy brought some iodine and some cornstarch to school. The iodine bottle was marked "poison." All bottles containing poison are marked like the picture.

"Cornstarch has starch in it," said Jimmy.

Mr. Thorne had Jimmy put some cornstarch and water into a test tube and shake it. "Now, let's see what iodine does to the starch," said Jimmy.

Jimmy put a drop of the dark-brown iodine into the test tube. The iodine turned the starch and water dark blue!

Mr. Thorne gave Jimmy some salt. Jimmy put the salt and some water into the test tube and shook it. When he added a drop of iodine, there was no change in color.

"I know how to test for starch now," said Jimmy. "If there is starch in food, iodine makes it a blue color. If starch is not there, the iodine does not make a blue color. Am I right, Mr. Thorne?"

"You had better test more than two substances before you make such a definite statement," said Mr. Thorne. "Scientists test many things carefully before they are sure of their results."

"All right," said Jimmy. "Let's test some of our vegetables."

He cut a thin slice of white potato and put it in a white dish with a little water. When he put iodine on it, the whole slice turned dark blue. "White potatoes have a lot of starch in them," he said.

"I want to test another stem," said Jimmy. "Wait just a minute," and he left the room. He was back very soon with several twigs in his hand.

"I cut these twigs from the maple tree and the elm tree in the yard," he said. "They are stems. Let's see if they contain stored food like the potato does."

He split the twigs with his knife and dropped iodine on the split surfaces. The iodine made a blue spot under each bud on the twigs. The thin layer under the bark turned blue, too.

"These twigs have stored starch," said Jimmy.

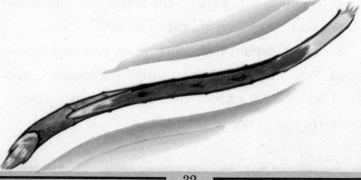

"Roots store food, too," said Susan. "Let's test some of our root vegetables."

Jimmy cut slices from a carrot, a beet, and a turnip. He tested them for starch. The iodine made only a few little dots of dark blue on each slice. "There isn't so much starch in carrots and beets and turnips as in the white potato," said Jimmy.

"How about the sweet potato?" asked Dick.

Jimmy cut a thin slice of sweet potato. He put it in a white dish and put iodine on it. "There is not so much starch in this sweet potato as there was in the white potato," he said.

"The carrots, beets, and sweet potato are already colored, Jimmy," said Mr. Thorne. "The blue does not show up as it does on the white potato. However, sweet potatoes contain another kind of food, also. Taste a piece."

Jimmy cut pieces of sweet potato for everybody. When Jane tasted her piece, she said, "It's sweet. Sweet potatoes must have sugar stored in them."

"I've heard that sugar is sometimes made from sugar beets," said Dick. "Is sugar stored in beets?"

"Yes," answered Mr. Thorne. "Sweet potatoes, beets, carrots, and turnips have some sugar stored in them."

Susan's Observation

After a few days Susan noticed that something had happened to the cabbage Mr. Baker had given them. It had been on a shelf in the closet. Now a sprout was growing from it.

"Look at this sprout," she called. "What made the cabbage sprout when it wasn't planted?"

"Our other experiments ought to help us answer that question," said Jane. "We found that plants have food stored in their roots and stems. The stored food helps the plants grow. The cabbage had stored food that helped it grow."

"Yes," said Mr. Thorne. "The thick stem inside the head of cabbage contains some food. The heavy leaves contain water and some food, also."

"I've seen sprouts on potatoes," said Dick. "The sprouts grow from the eyes. The stored food must help the sprouts grow."

"And I've seen sprouts on onions," said Nancy. "Last spring we had some onions in a bag in the cellar. When Mother sent me to get some, the bag was full of long green sprouts. The onions were soft. We couldn't use them."

"I remember how our narcissus bulbs got soft after they began to sprout and grow," said Susan.

"Did the onions and the narcissus bulbs get soft because the stored food went into the sprouts?" asked Dick.

"Yes," said Mr. Thorne. "When the stored food was used by the growing sprouts, the bulbs became soft. Sprouting potatoes are soft. This sprouting cabbage is soft, too."

Chemical Change

A few days after the experiments with foods Jane said, "Why did the iodine and starch turn blue?"

No one answered her.

"Can you tell us, Mr. Thorne?" asked Jane.

"I think I can help you find an answer," said Mr. Thorne.

"Has anyone ever seen anything else change color?" he asked.

"We used some blueprint paper that changed color," said Susan.

"Mother said the sun made her rug change color," said Bob.

"But iodine is not paper, or a rug," said Jane. "It's . . ." she stopped.

"You mean that iodine is a liquid," said Mr. Thorne.

"Yes, and it wasn't in the sun," said Jane. "We just put it on the starch and it turned blue. When we put it on sugar it didn't turn blue."

"The starch must have something in it that the sugar doesn't have," said Jimmy.

"The iodine and the blueprint paper aren't the

same," said Mr. Thorne, "but what happened to them was something alike."

"They both changed their color," said Bob.

"That's right," said Mr. Thorne.

"I have some liquids in my chemistry set," said Dick. "When I put two of them together they turn red."

"I have some invisible ink in my set," said Bob. "I write with it and you can't see it. When I paint what I have written with water, you can see it."

"Can you make it invisible again?" asked Mr. Thorne.

"No," said Bob. "It stays visible."

"Can you make the iodine change back to brown after it is blue?"

"No," said the children.

"We call that a *chemical change*," said Mr. Thorne. "Iodine is a chemical. How would you describe it?" Mr. Thorne wrote these things on the board as the children told him.

It is a liquid.

It is brown.

"A scientist would say that these are two of the *properties* of iodine. Properties are the ways by which you know something. For instance, how do you recognize salt?"

"It's white and tastes salty," said Nancy.

"Yes," said Mr. Thorne, "those are two properties of salt. Do you know any others?"

"It dissolves in water," said Jane.

"It makes crystals," said Jimmy.

"The crystals are square," said Bob.

"Those are three more properties of salt," said Mr. Thorne. "Do you remember what happened to the salt when you dissolved it?" he asked.

"It disappeared into the water," said Bob.

"When the water evaporated we got the salt again," said Jimmy.

"Yes, that's right," said Mr. Thorne. "The salt really didn't change its properties when it dissolved. Is that the same kind of change we had with the iodine?"

"No," said Bob. "The iodine was brown at first. When we put it on the starch it turned blue."

"That's right," said Mr. Thorne. "The properties of the iodine are not the same after it touches starch. There has been a chemical change."

The children wanted to find out about other chemicals. Mr. Thorne told them to look for chemical changes at home. He suggested that they might find chemicals in the kitchen.

The next day Nancy brought an example of chemical change. She had a half of a lemon and some soda. She sprinkled the soda in some of the lemon juice. It bubbled.

"You have caused a chemical change," said Mr. Thorne. "What are the properties of the lemon juice?" he asked.

"It's yellow."

"It's sour," said the children.

"How does it taste now, Nancy?" he asked.

Nancy tasted the juice.

"It doesn't taste sour," she said.

"No," said Mr. Thorne. "The soda changed the properties of the lemon juice."

"My mother puts soda in sour milk," said Jane.

"What happens?" asked Mr. Thorne.

"It foams," said Jane.

"That is a chemical change," said Mr. Thorne. "Your mother would say she was sweetening the milk. Scientists have a name for chemicals like lemon juice. Scientists call such sour chemicals *acids*."

"But I thought chemicals were poisonous," said Bob.

"Some of them are," said Mr. Thorne, "but many of them are common things we use every day, like salt and soda."

"We used an acid to test limestone," said Jimmy. "We couldn't taste that. How do you know it's an acid?"

"It fizzed when we put it on the limestone," said Bob.

"There is a better way to tell an acid," said Mr. Thorne. He went to the cupboard and brought back a little bottle. In the bottle were some strips of blue paper.

"There is some juice left in your lemon, Nancy," he said. "Squeeze a little onto a piece of this paper."

Nancy squeezed some lemon juice onto a strip of the blue paper. "Oh, the paper has turned pink!" she said.

"It caused a chemical change," the children said. "What kind of paper is that?"

"It is a special kind of paper," said Mr. Thorne. "It is called blue litmus paper. It has a chemical called litmus in it. When an acid touches the litmus it causes a chemical change. The blue paper turns pink."

All the children wanted to test something with the blue litmus paper. Mr. Thorne suggested that each of them bring something to school the next day. They would test the things they brought.

The next day the children tested many things with the blue litmus paper. These are some of the things that were not acid.

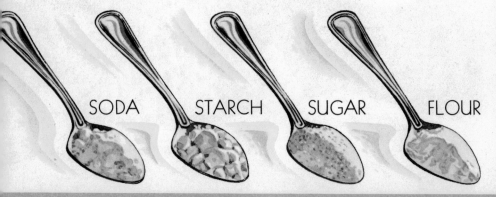

SODA   STARCH   SUGAR   FLOUR

These are some of the things that were acid:

      Orange   Grapefruit

      Tomato   Apple

      Vinegar

The children wrote in their notebooks:

Acids are chemicals.

Acids are sour. They turn blue litmus paper pink.

How Beavers Live

"Hal, Hal," called Jack.

Cowboy Hal stopped his horse while Jack galloped up to him. Jack was breathing fast and looked excited. "Somebody has been in our woods and cut down a lot of young poplar trees. Whoever it was hasn't taken them away yet. They are lying along the bank of the stream."

"Let's have a look at them," said Cowboy Hal.

They rode back along the stream to the edge of the woods. The stream was shallow at this point, but it was almost fifteen feet wide. Sure enough, many young poplar trees had been cut down.

"I wish we could catch the fellow who cut them," said Jack. "It's a shame to kill fine young trees like this."

"I don't think you'd really want to catch him if you knew who he was," said Cowboy Hal. "It wasn't a man who cut these trees. It was an animal with brown fur. It was a beaver."

Jack jumped off his horse. He looked carefully at several of the stumps. They had been cut very neatly.

"The beaver must have wonderful teeth," said Jack. "These chips look something like the chips that an axe makes. And look, Hal, almost every one of these trees has fallen in the same direction. The tops of most of them are touching the water."

"The beavers are going to pull the trees out into the water and use them to build a new lodge," said Cowboy Hal.

"Let's watch them build their lodge," said Jack.

"They won't build it while we are here," said Cowboy Hal. "We'd better move along. Would you like to see a beaver lodge that is already built?"

"Yes, I would," said Jack.

A hundred yards up the stream Jack and Cowboy Hal came to a beaver dam. Above the dam was a big pond. All around the bank of the pond were

stumps of trees. The stumps looked like those Jack had already found.

"Did the beavers cut all these trees, too?" asked Jack.

"Yes, indeed," said Cowboy Hal.

"Beavers are certainly interesting animals," said Jack. "Tell me more about them."

"They're as interesting as any animals we have in this country," said Cowboy Hal. "Two years ago this pond wasn't here. Then the beavers came; they cut down all these trees.

"They cut the branches off the trees. They cut the trees into pieces they could move. Then they put these pieces into the stream one by one, and put little branches, twigs, and grass and mud in the cracks to stop up the water. That's what made this dam. Look, you can see how it is made."

By this time Jack and Cowboy Hal were close to the dam. Jack could see that it was a strong one. It was almost eight feet thick at the bottom, four feet high, and long enough to reach across the stream. Very little water leaked between the twigs and branches in the dam.

In the deepest part of the pond, there were two piles of mud and sticks. They were about six feet high. They looked like little islands.

"Those piles of mud and sticks," continued Cowboy Hal, "are the beavers' lodges, and this pond is their playground."

"The lodges look like the mud huts of some of the Indians who live on the plains," said Jack. "But I don't see any doorways in them. How do the beavers get in and out?"

"Their doors are under the water," said Cowboy Hal. "The beavers' enemies can't swim under water as the beavers can; the hidden doorways protect the beavers from unwelcome visitors."

Cowboy Hal took a scrap of paper from his pocket and drew a picture. "Look here! If you could see into a beaver's lodge, it would look like this.

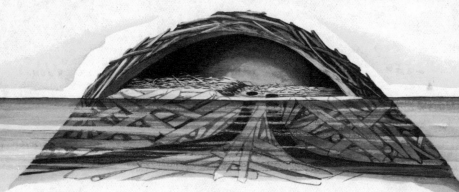

"The walls of a lodge are usually about a foot thick. They are made of sticks and mud. When the mud freezes in cold weather, the walls become very strong. Only a bear with its sharp claws or a man with a pick and shovel could break through.

"The beavers are well protected in their strongly built lodges. They live in a room which is above the level of the water. Here they can keep warm and dry. Their room is large enough so that a boy could sit in it."

"Beavers are smart animals, aren't they?" said Jack as he studied the picture.

"What do beavers eat?" was his next question.

"Usually they eat roots and stems of plants. Where the water is shallow and calm in the beaver ponds, water lilies and cat-tails grow. The beavers are fond of food like that. The food they like best, though, comes from willow and poplar trees. They eat the bark and the layer of starch under the bark. Starch is good food for beavers as well as for you."

"But what happens when the pond freezes in the winter?" asked Jack.

"The beavers don't have to come out of the pond," answered Cowboy Hal. "They store all the food that they will need during the winter in the pond. See all the trees they have cut."

Jack counted. He could count nearly a hundred stumps.

"I see where the beavers' food is now," said Jack. "It is in the dam. The trees they cut are in the dam. When they need food, the beavers just swim to the dam and eat some of the bark. After they have had their meal, they swim back and crawl up into their warm houses again."

"Sometimes they eat bark from branches in the dam," said Cowboy Hal. "But most of their food is stored in the pond. They cut some of the trees into pieces and store them near their lodges."

"Beavers go to a lot of trouble to store their food," said Jack. "How many beavers do you think live in this pond?"

"I'm not sure of the exact number," said Cowboy Hal. "There are two lodges. There are probably two male beavers and their mates. That makes four. Each family may have had from two to five young beavers. There may be as many as fourteen beavers here, or as few as eight."

"Do beavers always live together in ponds like this?" asked Jack.

"Yes," said Cowboy Hal. "They can make larger and stronger dams when there are more beavers to do the work. The male beavers usually cut the trees and trim off the branches. They put the trees into place in the dam and help build the lodges.

After the young beavers are born, the mothers take care of them. They won't let the young beavers leave the pond until they are a year old."

"Suppose the beavers eat all the food they have stored. What will they do the next winter?"

"They will cut down more trees. When all the trees on the banks are gone, the beavers will enlarge their pond by digging canals. Over there is a canal," said Cowboy Hal. "The beavers can swim to other trees. When the trees are cut, they can be floated to the dam along the canals. It is easier and safer to float trees than to drag them."

"I'd like to see a beaver at work," said Jack.

"Not many people have seen beavers working," said Cowboy Hal. "Beavers do most of their work at night. Maybe if we go down tonight to the place where those new trees are cut, and lie very still, we will see how busy beavers can be."

"Why are the beavers building a new dam?" asked Jack.

"The new dam will make a pond that will probably be the home of the young beavers which are just mating. Their parents will stay back in the old pond and probably live there all their lives."

As soon as Jack and Cowboy Hal had finished their supper, they put on warm coats and went back to the stream where the new beaver dam was being built. When they were near the cut trees, they got down on their hands and knees and crawled very quietly. Then they lay perfectly still. Jack was almost afraid to breathe for fear he would make too much noise. Soon a beaver glided silently out of the water. For a moment its wet hair glistened in the moonlight. Then it seemed all dry again.

"The beaver has two kinds of fur," whispered Cowboy Hal. "Next to its body is a heavy coat of short soft hair that never gets wet. The long brown hair on the outside sheds the water."

The beaver was a clumsy animal. It waddled from side to side and moved slowly. It came right toward the tree in front of Jack and Cowboy Hal. It stood up with its front feet against the tree. It was almost three feet tall. Jack thought it must weigh about fifty pounds. Its tail was broad and flat and helped the beaver balance itself when it stood on its hind legs.

Again Cowboy Hal whispered, "The beaver uses its tail when it swims. The broad flat surface acts like a rudder on a boat. It helps steer the body."

First the beaver gnawed a line around the tree trunk. Then it cut another line around the tree trunk about six inches below the first line. Then it began to gnaw out the wood between the two circles. The tree began to look like the one in the picture.

The beaver cut more deeply into the tree on the side nearest the stream. When it had worked steadily for about twenty minutes, the tree trunk was almost cut through. Jack was afraid the tree would fall and crush the little fellow. But there was no need to worry. The beaver knew its business. It stood on its hind legs and pushed the tree as hard as it could. Slowly the tree swayed. The beaver thumped the ground with its tail to warn near-by beavers that the tree was going to fall. Then the top branches splashed into the water.

The beaver didn't even take a rest. It went right to work to cut the branches off the tree. Then it cut the tree in two. With its front feet, it dragged one part at a time into the water.

Just then Jack sneezed. *Slap!* went the beaver's tail on the water and the beaver disappeared.

"That ends tonight's fun," said Cowboy Hal. "When a beaver slaps its tail on the water like that, it means *Danger! Hide!* There won't be any more beavers out here for a long while; we might as well go home."

"You were right, Hal. Beavers are certainly interesting," said Jack as they started for home. "They can do many things. They cut trees like real woodsmen. They build houses as well as carpenters do. Their dams are as strong and tight as the dams that men build."

"And don't forget that the male beavers are good fathers, too. They store enough food to last all winter for their families," said Cowboy Hal.

"Are there any other animals that live the way beavers live?" asked Jack.

"Yes," said Cowboy Hal, "the beaver's cousin, the muskrat, lives in much the same way as the beaver. The muskrat is smaller than the beaver but except for its tail it looks very much the same."

"Muskrats usually build their homes in the banks of streams," Cowboy Hal went on. "The entrances to their homes are under the water, too. Sometimes muskrats will build lodges of cat-tail stems. They look much like the ones beavers build. Muskrats eat stems of cat-tails and the roots of plants."

"The stems of cat-tails aren't so tough as the trunks of willow trees," said Jack. "Don't the muskrats have as strong teeth as the beavers?"

"The muskrats' teeth are not so large as the beavers' teeth, but otherwise they are like them. In the stable I have an old beaver's skull that you have never seen. The teeth are still in place. You can see for yourself what they look like when we get home."

Other Gnawing Animals

Cowboy Hal brought his box of skulls into the house to show Jack. He put them on the table.

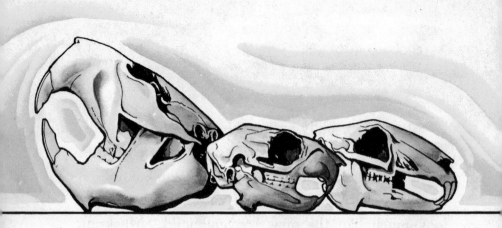

"That first one on the left is a beaver's skull."

"Whew! those front teeth are big and sharp!" said Jack, when he felt them. "When the upper teeth come down over the lower ones, they can snap twigs off just like scissors, can't they?"

"As a matter of fact," said Cowboy Hal, "they are called *incisors* or scissor teeth. The beaver gnaws the bark off the trees with its incisors. It grinds the food with its back teeth."

Jack picked up the middle skull. "This must be a young beaver's skull," he said.

"Wrong," said Cowboy Hal, "that skull came from a full-grown squirrel, and this last one came from a rabbit."

"But the teeth are almost the same," said Jack. "Rabbits and squirrels don't have to cut trees. Why do they have these long incisors?"

"I'm glad you called the front teeth incisors," said Cowboy Hal. "Call things by their exact names when you know them. Rabbits sometimes eat bark of young trees, but they also gnaw roots and stems of plants to get their food. They gnaw cabbages, carrots, and turnips — any of the parts of green plants where food is stored. Animals that gnaw the food stored in plants are called *rodents*. Beavers are rodents. Squirrels are rodents. Rabbits are related to beavers and squirrels."

"I've seen rabbits gnaw carrots," said Jack. "Their teeth make marks on carrots like the beavers' teeth make on tree trunks. Don't they have any tearing teeth like dogs and cats?"

"No," said Cowboy Hal, "most rodents don't eat meat. Tearing teeth, or *canine* teeth, as they are called, are used only by animals that eat meat."

"It seems queer that a rabbit belongs to a group of animals that live in the water, like beavers," said Jack.

"Even rats and mice belong to the rodent group," said Cowboy Hal. "They have strong incisors, too. Having gnawing teeth is only one way in which rats, mice, and rabbits are like beavers, though. The beavers, you remember, store their food. They also build very comfortable houses to live in. Rats, mice, and rabbits do neither of these things. They do not store food. They dig very simple holes in the ground or live in brush piles or other simple shelters. They don't store their food in their burrows. They have to hunt for food every day. Sometimes the food becomes so scarce near their homes in the woods that they have to come nearer to men's houses. Then they are in danger from men and dogs."

"But squirrels store food, don't they, Hal?" asked Jack.

"Yes, they do," said Cowboy Hal. "Squirrels and chipmunks always collect food and store it even if they are pets and are being fed.

"Once I had a little red squirrel that I raised right here in the house. When I gave it nuts, it used to hide them under pillows and in corners. Squirrels that live out of doors store their food in many places. Their nests are usually in holes in trees. Some squirrels make nests of leaves. They store some of their winter food in their nests, but they hide more of it in holes in buildings and in the ground. It is natural for squirrels to collect and hide food. They do not have to learn to do either."

"I've seen squirrels digging in the ground in the fall," said Jack. "Were they burying their food?"

"They probably were," said Cowboy Hal. "In the winter those same squirrels will try to find the nuts they've buried. They won't be able to find all of them, of course. Other squirrels may have already found some of them. Sometimes when the nuts are left in the ground until spring, they sprout and grow into trees."

"I don't think I ever saw a squirrel when there was snow on the ground," said Jack.

"When the weather is bad, squirrels usually stay in their warm nests in the trees," said Cowboy Hal. "They come out in winter only on sunshiny days. Chipmunks act in almost the same way. They make nests in hollow trees or in the ground. They dig tunnels eight or ten feet long, and then hollow out big rooms for themselves. They line their rooms with leaves and grass and stock them with nuts and grain. Sometimes they begin storing their food in the middle of the summer. When the cold days come, they curl up in their nests and don't come out again until spring."

"Then chipmunks hibernate, don't they?" asked Jack.

"No, they don't hibernate the way woodchucks do," said Cowboy Hal. "Chipmunks wake up often during the winter months. They eat a good meal. Then they go back to sleep again. Animals that hibernate don't eat anything at all during the winter."

"I should think that the teeth of rodents would soon wear away," said Jack. "They gnaw on very hard food. Squirrels and chipmunks even gnaw nuts to get their food."

"That is one of the remarkable things about rodents," said Cowboy Hal. "Their incisor teeth are really growing all the time. They grow as fast as they are worn off. As a matter of fact, if rodents didn't have hard food to gnaw, their incisors would grow so long that they couldn't eat."

"But don't their teeth ever wear dull?" asked Jack.

"No," said Cowboy Hal. "The back part of their teeth is softer than the front part. The back part wears away more quickly and leaves a sharp edge all the time."

"Are my teeth like that?" asked Jack. "Will my teeth always keep themselves sharpened?"

Cowboy Hal laughed, "Oh, no, my boy; after your teeth come in they stop growing. You had one set of baby teeth. Now your permanent teeth are growing. By the time you are fourteen, you will have almost all of them. They are the last ones you will have. You should take good care of them."

"I try to take care of them," said Jack. "I brush them every day. I go to see the dentist twice a year. I'm going to see him again next week. I'm going to ask him to tell me all about my teeth. I know about the teeth of many animals. I'd like to know about my own."

Jack wanted to be sure of all the things he knew about animals' teeth. He wrote these sentences in his notebook:

1. I know that cows and sheep eat grass.
    They do not have incisors in their upper jaws.
    They cut grass with their strong tongues.
    They have large teeth at the back to grind their food.

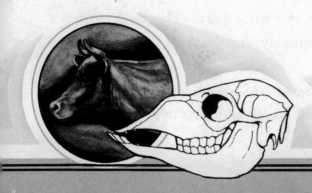

2. I know that dogs and cats eat meat.
   All of their teeth are pointed.
   They have small incisors in both jaws.
   They have long, sharp canine teeth to tear their
     meat.
   They have grinding teeth to
     help them crush bones.

3. I know that rodents gnaw their food.
   They have very strong incisors. The incisors
     help them gnaw their food.
   They have no canine teeth.
   They do not often eat meat.
   They have grinding teeth at
     the back to help them grind
     their food.

4. I think all animals must have special kinds of
     teeth that help them eat the food they need.

Different Kinds of Teeth

Jack didn't mind going to the dentist's office. He was anxious to find out all he could about his teeth. When the dentist had finished examining Jack's teeth, he said, "Your teeth are in excellent condition, Jack. You must have cleaned them every day. They look healthy, too. Plenty of milk, fruit, and green vegetables help keep them in good condition."

"Would you please take a few minutes to tell me about my teeth?" asked Jack. "I've been learning about the teeth of many animals. I would like to know more about my own."

"I'll be glad to," said the dentist. "Here is a model of a man's tooth. You may examine it."

"This looks like the canine teeth that dogs and cats use to tear their meat," said Jack.

"It is a man's canine tooth. Men eat meat, too," said the dentist. "This hard white covering is enamel. This part is the root of the tooth. The roots go into the jaw. Look in the mirror and see if you can find your canine teeth."

Jack found four canine teeth—two in each jaw.

In front, between the canine teeth in each jaw, there were four teeth.

"Are these sharp front teeth incisors?" he asked.

"Yes," said the dentist. "You have eight incisors, four in the upper jaw and four in the lower."

"But I don't gnaw my food as rodents do. Why do I have incisors?" he asked.

"You do gnaw some of your food," said the dentist. "Think of how you eat corn off the cob."

"That's right," laughed Jack. "I gnaw it just as a squirrel gnaws a nut."

"Why do you have to pull teeth for people?" asked Jack.

"Not all people eat the kind of food that keeps their teeth in good condition," said the dentist. "Not all people clean their teeth every day. If people do not clean their teeth, pieces of food stay between the teeth and form an acid which makes holes in the enamel. Then the teeth decay."

"Couldn't you repair the bad teeth instead of pulling them out?" asked Jack.

"Yes," said the dentist, "if people come to me soon enough, I put something hard in the cavity. I put in a filling. The filling keeps the acid from destroying the roots of the tooth. In another year or two you will have all your permanent teeth. You must take good care of them. One of my patients did not take good care of his teeth. I had to pull all of them out. This is a set of teeth I have made for him."

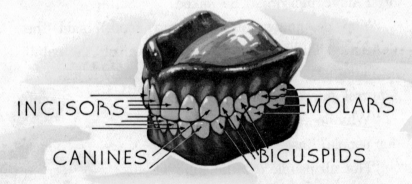

"These at the back are grinding teeth, aren't they?" asked Jack.

"Yes," said the dentist. "But the correct name for them is *molars*. These eight small grinders are called *bicuspids*. There are eight incisors, four canine teeth, eight bicuspids, and eight molars. That makes twenty-eight. Some people have four more molars. They are called *wisdom* teeth. That makes thirty-two. The wisdom teeth of some people never grow."

"What should I clean my teeth with to keep them from decaying?" asked Jack.

"The most important thing is to remove the food from between your teeth," said the dentist. "A toothbrush will help do that. Dental floss also helps. You should use dental floss every day. When you pull it between your teeth, it takes out all the food. If you want to make something to clean your teeth with, put a little soda and some salt into a glass of water. There isn't anything better for cleaning your teeth."

"Thank you," said Jack. "You have given me a lot of helpful information about my teeth."

When Jack got home, he added these sentences in his notebook:

5. I have eight incisors. I can gnaw food.
   I have four canine teeth. I can tear food.
   I have sixteen grinding teeth. I can grind food.

6. Men have three kinds of teeth. Men can eat all kinds of food.

A Spider's Bridge

One morning Ted and Joyce went out early with Uncle Don. They went to the park along the bank of the river. Ted and Joyce live in a large city. One of their favorite places is the park.

The air was clear and cool in the early morning. It was fun to draw deep breaths of fresh air.

"Oh! Uncle Don, isn't it great to be out of doors so early?" asked Ted.

Just then Ted looked up the river and saw two very high towers, one on each side of the river. The towers seemed to reach almost as high as the clouds. The children looked at them in amazement. The towers had not been there when they last visited the park.

"What are those towers, Uncle Don?" asked Ted.

"They are the beginning of one of the longest suspension bridges in the world," said Uncle Don.

"Suspension bridge," said Ted. "Why do you call it a *suspension* bridge?"

"It is called a suspension bridge because it will be suspended or hung from those two towers," replied Uncle Don.

Ted and Joyce could scarcely believe that a bridge could be stretched across so wide a river. Just then the children noticed two big ropes attached to the towers. They swung in graceful curves across the river.

"Will the bridge be attached to those ropes, Uncle Don?" asked Ted.

"Yes," said Uncle Don, "but those aren't just ropes. They are cables made of many strands of strong wire."

"Look," cried both the children at once. "There is something crawling across the cables. What is it, Uncle Don? Watch it!"

"It's going very slowly," said Ted.

"It's a wheel," said Joyce.

"Yes," said Uncle Don, "the workmen call it the traveler wheel."

"Does it carry anything?" asked Joyce.

"Yes, it is carrying another strand of wire to make the big cable stronger. It goes back and forth, back and forth, until it has carried thousands of strands of wire," said Uncle Don.

Ted was still looking at the moving wheel without saying a word. He seemed puzzled. Suddenly he said, "I think it looks like a spider."

"Ugh! A spider!" said Joyce.

"It does look like a spider," agreed Uncle Don. "And it does the same kind of work that a spider does."

"How could a spider make a bridge like that?" asked Joyce. "Spiders make webs, not bridges."

"Some people think that spiders are the best bridge builders in the world," said Uncle Don.

"Let's see if we can find a spider," said Ted. "I'd like to see one work."

"Here's a web on this bush," said Joyce. "See how it glistens in the sun just like silk threads."

"And here's a spider over here. Quick! See! It's sitting on that leaf. It's almost the same color as the leaf. We're lucky to find it," said Ted.

Just then the spider seemed to stand up a little higher on its legs. The children thought it was going to run away. Instead, it dropped from the leaf on a thread of silk.

"Uncle Don, how does a spider spin its silk?" asked Joyce.

"How does a caterpillar spin its silk?" asked Uncle Don.

"A caterpillar has little openings under its mouth," said Joyce. "The silk comes from them."

"True," said Uncle Don. "And the spider has little tubes under the back part of its body. The back part of its body is called its *abdomen*. These little tubes in the abdomen are called *spinnerets*. With its spinnerets the spider spins threads. Spiders make yards and yards of fine silk threads."

The silk thread grew longer and longer. When it reached almost to the ground, the spider stopped spinning and swung in the air.

"What's the spider waiting for now, Uncle Don? Will it run up to the leaf?" asked Ted.

"Let's watch and see," said Uncle Don. "The thread is swinging a little now. Watch closely."

Just then a breeze blew the spider several feet. It was almost straight out. It touched another leaf and stayed there.

Immediately the spider began to walk back on the thread. Its feet clung to the thread as the spider moved upside-down along its bridge.

"Uncle Don is right," cried Ted. "That thread is just like a bridge. The spider is crossing it now, just as the wheel crossed the cable."

"Look!" said Ted. "The thread is thicker where the spider has walked. It's making another thread of silk as it goes along."

"Yes," said Uncle Don. "It is making the top of its web. Spiders always make the tops of their webs first. They make the tops stronger so that they will hold all the other threads."

"What do spiders eat?" asked Joyce.

"They feed on insects," said Uncle Don. "They kill more flies than anything else. Flies help spread disease. When spiders kill flies they are a benefit to man."

"Flies move much faster than spiders can," said Ted. "How can the spiders catch them?"

"A spider doesn't chase flies," said Uncle Don. "Flies are caught in the spider's web. The silk threads are sticky like fly paper and hold the insects fast. Then the spider winds a few more threads around the fly's body to hold it still. When the fly can't move, the spider bites it. Then the spider sucks the fly's blood."

"Would a spider bite us, Uncle Don?" asked Ted.

"Sometimes a spider will bite, but it would probably not poison you," said Uncle Don. "There is only one kind of spider in the United States that is poisonous to man. It is the Black Widow Spider."

"Do you suppose we'll find one around here?" asked Joyce.

"We might," said Uncle Don, "but Black Widow Spiders usually live in hot, dry climates. They are rare in this part of the country."

"What does a Black Widow look like?" asked Ted.

"It is not a very big spider. The female is all black except for one bright red spot under her abdomen."

"Are there many different kinds of spiders?" asked Joyce.

"Indeed there are," said Uncle Don. "There are hundreds of kinds. Some of them do interesting things. This one you are looking at belongs to the orb-weaver group. The orb-weavers make webs like this one we just found.

"The Golden Garden Spider belongs to the orb-weaver group. This spider makes a glider."

"I know what a glider is," said Joyce. "Ted has one. It is an airplane that flies without a motor."

"You have the right idea," said Uncle Don. "In the spring the young Golden Garden Spiders climb to high twigs and spin silk threads. When the wind blows, the spiders float off on their silken gliders to new homes."

"How far do they go?" asked Joyce.

"Sometimes they make long trips," said Uncle Don. "A few of them have floated over the ocean. They have reached islands hundreds of miles away."

"That sounds like the story of the magic carpet," said Ted. "Do Golden Garden Spiders make webs, too?"

"Indeed they do," said Uncle Don. "They make webs that look like the one of this orb-weaver."

"The grass spiders just spin sheets of silk on the grass," continued Uncle Don. "They make their webs look like empty ice cream cones. They hide at the bottom of the cones. The insects fall right into the spiders' houses."

"My! Spiders are interesting insects," said Joyce.

"Ho!" laughed Ted. "A spider isn't an insect!"

"Why isn't it an insect?" asked Joyce.

"Count its legs," said Ted. "It has eight legs."

Then Joyce remembered that insects have only six legs. She looked at the spider more closely. "I was wrong about its legs, but I see something else. A spider's body has only two sections. An insect's body has three sections."

"That's fine, Joyce," said Uncle Don. "Now you know a second difference between spiders and insects."

"Do spiders lay eggs?" asked Joyce.

"Yes, they do," said Uncle Don.

"What do young spiders look like?" asked Joyce.

"They look like their parents when they are hatched," answered Uncle Don. "Insects do not look like their parents when they are hatched."

"That's the third difference between spiders and insects," cried Ted. "I remember how mosquitoes grow from wigglers."

"Good for you," said Uncle Don. "This grass spider lays many eggs. It hides the eggs in dark places. It hides them under rocks and in wood piles. It puts a lot of eggs together and wraps them in silk threads something like a cocoon. When the little spiders hatch in the egg cases, there isn't room for all of them. Some of the little spiders eat some of the other little spiders. As they grow larger they become stronger. By spring they are able to break the egg case and come out. Then they are big enough to spin their own webs and catch their own food."

More About Spiders

Ted and Joyce were so interested in spiders that they went to the library to learn more about them. They found many books and pictures. It was fun to read about spiders. They soon had many things to tell Uncle Don.

"Uncle Don," said Joyce, "we found out that not all spiders spin webs to catch their food."

"That's interesting," said Uncle Don. "Tell me about them."

"One is a Crab Spider," said Joyce. "In the early summer it hides in white flowers. In the summer the spider is all white, too. At the end of the summer it goes to live on the goldenrod. Its color changes then. It turns yellow."

"I suppose its color protects it," said Uncle Don.

"Yes," said Joyce. "When spiders are the same color as the plants they live on, their enemies can't see them. Their color protects them. The Crab Spider is protected in another way. Sometimes it crawls inside flowers. It pulls the petals over its head. The petals are like a tent. The Crab Spider hides under its tent."

"If it doesn't make a web, how does it catch its food?" asked Uncle Don.

"It hides on the flower or under the petals until an insect comes along. Then it runs sidewise like a crab and kills the insect."

"I learned about a jumping spider," said Ted. "It doesn't make a web either. It lives on tree trunks and posts. Sometimes it lives on the stems of plants or on the outside of buildings."

"What does it look like?" asked Uncle Don.

"It is brightly colored," said Ted. "It has short legs and big eyes."

"Why is it called a jumping spider, Ted?" asked Uncle Don.

"It is a good jumper," said Ted. "It jumps on its food. It can jump forward; it can jump sidewise; it can jump backward. Every time it jumps it spins a thread. It can follow the thread back to where it started from, so it never gets lost."

"It sounds like a mighty smart spider to me," laughed Uncle Don. "I know about another smart spider. Did you read about the Trap Door Spider?"

"No," said Ted, "but tell us about it. It sounds interesting."

"Well," said Uncle Don. "Trap Door Spiders don't make webs either. They live in the ground. They dig long tunnels and line them with silk."

"What about the trap door?" asked Ted.

"The trap door is at the entrance to the tunnel. The spider can open and close it. When the spider is inside, it can hold the door so tight that no other spider or insect can open it. The spider is well protected from its enemies."

"How does the Trap Door Spider get its food?" asked Joyce.

"The spider hides in its nest. It pushes the door up a little and watches for an insect. When an insect comes close enough, the spider jumps out and catches it."

"I'd like to see a Trap Door Spider sometime," said Ted.

"Maybe you will," said Uncle Don. "It belongs to the Tarantula family. Most of the spiders that live in the ground belong to the Tarantula family. Some Tarantulas are very large."

"Aren't Tarantulas dangerous?" asked Joyce.

"No," said Uncle Don. "Tarantulas do not often bite human beings. And their bite isn't serious. Spiders are really useful animals. They are helpful to man. They eat many insects that are harmful to man."

Plants Depend on Animals

Martha Lou and Randy live in the South where it seldom snows. They do not have cold winter days. They can play outside almost every day. Nearly every day of the year is warm. Most of the trees stay green all the year round. Many of the trees have leaves in winter as well as in summer.

Martha Lou and Randy live on a large plantation. The plantation is on the low land near a wide, slow-moving river. Their father raises sugar cane and cotton. He raises vegetables and fruit, too.

Martha Lou and Randy like best the strawberries that their father raises. The berries are big, sweet ones that grow while it is very cold in the northern part of the United States. Martha Lou's and Randy's father sells strawberries. People in the North buy them.

Their father also raises bees. Martha Lou and Randy learned that if they didn't bother the bees the bees wouldn't bother them. But one day as they were playing, they disturbed a hive of bees quite by accident.

"Oh-h-h-h-h!" cried Martha Lou. "My fingers! I'm stung!"

Bees by the hundreds swarmed through the air.

"Let's get to the house!" cried Randy. Both children ran as fast as they could.

"Mother! Mother!" cried Martha Lou. "The bees are after us!"

The children ran into the house and quickly shut the door.

Mother looked at Martha Lou's swollen fingers. "I'll put some baking soda on them," she said. "Baking soda will make your fingers feel better."

"Oh, dear!" sobbed Martha Lou. "Every place we want to play always has bees in it. The barn has bees in it! The garden is always full of bees! Bees are everywhere. I don't see why they had to sting me!"

"But you disturbed a hive. The hive is the bees' home," Mother reminded her. "The bees have stored their honey in the hive. Honey is food for the bees, Martha Lou. Honey is food for you, too."

"Yes," agreed Martha Lou doubtfully. "But why couldn't we buy honey? Then we wouldn't have to have bees."

"Not have bees!" exclaimed Mother. "But bees are very important insects. Without bees we could not have such good strawberries. Our other fruit would not be so good, either."

The children were surprised. "How do bees help make good fruit?" they both asked at once.

"The bees get nectar from the flowers," said Mother. "Nectar is a sweet juice that many flowers have in them. Bees make their honey out of nectar. As the bees get the nectar, their legs brush against the pollen that is in the flowers. Some of the pollen sticks to their legs."

"What is pollen?" asked Martha Lou.

"Pollen is the fine yellow dust that grows in the centers of flowers. You have seen it on flowers, I know. Sometimes when you smell flowers, the pollen gets on your nose!

"The bees carry pollen from one flower to another," continued Mother. "Good fruit can not grow from the flowers of some plants unless the pollen from other plants is brought to them. The bees carry the pollen from one strawberry blossom to another."

"The bees help make good strawberries," said Martha Lou. "Without the bees we could not grow such good strawberries."

Animals Depend on Plants

That night at the dinner table, Martha Lou and Randy told their father about their experience with the bees.

"I guess we couldn't get along very well without bees," said Randy. "It does seem queer, though, that plants depend on them."

"Bees depend on plants, too," said Martha Lou. "If there were no flowers, the bees could get no nectar. Then they could make no honey. Bees and plants seem to need each other."

"Bees and plants do need each other," said Father. "Did you ever stop to think how much everything in this world depends on something else?"

"No, I guess I never did," said Randy.

"Animals of all kinds depend on plants," said Father. "*You* depend on plants. Plants give you food."

"That's right!" said Randy. "Look at all the plants we are eating for dinner! Sweet potatoes and corn and beans! Tomatoes, too!"

"And we're going to have watermelon for dessert!" laughed Martha Lou.

"If it weren't for plants, we wouldn't have much dinner!" said Randy.

He looked thoughtfully at the food on the table.

"Suppose there weren't a plant left on the earth," he went on. "What would we use for food?"

"Beefsteak!" said Martha Lou promptly.

"Wrong!" said Randy. "Beefsteak comes from cattle. Cattle eat grass and corn. Grass and corn are plants. Can you think of something else?"

"Fish," said Martha Lou.

"Wrong again!" laughed Randy. "Even our goldfish eat plants."

"We could eat honey," said Martha Lou. "Oh, of course not. Bees eat nectar and nectar comes from plants. How about cheese?"

"That's wrong, too," said Randy. "Cheese is made from milk and milk comes from cows. Cows live on plants!"

"We could eat eggs," said Martha Lou.

"No," said Randy. "Chickens lay eggs and chickens eat plants."

Martha Lou laughed. "We couldn't live without plants."

"Animals of all kinds depend on plants for food," said Father.

"I can see that animals depend on plants," said Randy. "I can see that plants need bees. But I can't see why plants need other animals."

"A good many plants are helped by animals," explained Father. "Plants grow in soil. The soil has materials in it that plants need. If plants use a great many of these materials, we farmers put fertilizer on the soil. Fertilizer contains materials plants can use. Fertilizer makes the soil richer because it puts into the soil the materials that plants need. Plants grow better when the soil is rich."

"I know what fertilizer is," said Randy. "Manure is fertilizer. Manure comes from the barnyard. The horses and cows and chickens make the manure."

"There are many kinds of fertilizer," said Father. "Some fertilizer comes from animals. Some fertilizer comes from plants. The roots or leaves of the plants are sometimes left in the fields. The farmers plow the leaves or roots into the ground. The roots and leaves decay and become fertilizer. Other farmers use certain kinds of chemicals for fertilizer. But the most common fertilizer is manure."

"Now I understand what you mean when you say that plants depend on animals," said Randy. Martha Lou nodded. She understood, too.

"Plants and animals depend on each other in another way," said Father. "Come. I will show you." He led the way to the sun porch. "The fish in our aquarium depend on plants."

"Fish eat plants," said Randy. "They use the plants for food."

"Fish use plants in another way," said Father. "Fish are animals. All animals need air to breathe. Where do fish get air to breathe?"

"Out of the water," said Randy. "There is some air in water. Fish can use the air that is in water."

"What is air made of?" asked Martha Lou. "We can feel it, but we can't see it. Why?"

"We can't see air because it is made of gases that we can't see," said Father. "The gas in the air which we use when we breathe is called *oxygen*. All animals must have oxygen to live. You must have oxygen; horses must have oxygen; dogs must have oxygen; and . . ."

"Fish must have oxygen," put in Randy.

"That is right," said Father. "Fish must have oxygen. There is some air in the water, as you said. But the fish soon use all the oxygen in the water. More oxygen must be added to the water so that the fish can live. This is where plants are useful. Green plants give off oxygen. Most fish live in lakes or streams where there are green plants. These plants give off oxygen. The fish breathe that oxygen. When we put fish into an aquarium, we must put plants into it also. The plants give off oxygen and the fish breathe it."

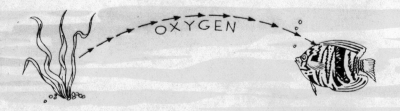

"But the story isn't over yet," Father went on. "The fish depend on plants for food and oxygen. But the plants depend on the fish, too."

"Do fish give off a gas, too?" laughed Randy.

"That's just what they do," said ·Father. "Fish breathe in oxygen. After their bodies have used the oxygen, they breathe out another gas. We can't see this gas, either. It is called *carbon dioxide*. Green plants use the carbon dioxide which the fish breathe out. They use it to make their food."

"Ho!" laughed Randy. "There's no end to this story. It goes round and round!"

"That's right," said Father. "It goes on in a circle. The fish depend on plants for food and oxygen. The plants depend on the fish for carbon dioxide."

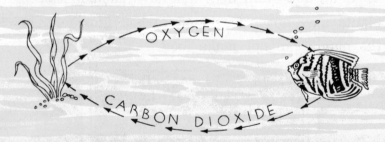

"That's why an aquarium should have both fish and green plants, isn't it?" asked Randy.

"Yes," answered Father. "An aquarium should always have enough green plants to give the right amount of food and oxygen for the fish. It should also have enough fish to give the right amount of carbon dioxide for the plants. If an aquarium has the right amount of plants, animals, water and air, we say it is *balanced*. Our aquarium is balanced.

"If an aquarium does not have enough green plants, the fish do not get enough oxygen. The fish are not healthy. They may die.

"If an aquarium does not have enough fish, the plants may not get enough carbon dioxide. Then the plants can not make food."

"Think of using carbon dioxide to make food!" said Martha Lou. "A gas doesn't sound very filling!"

"Yet it's the very thing which helps plants grow," said Father. "Plants use minerals from the soil, too, but the carbon dioxide from the air is very important. Plants combine the carbon dioxide with water to make starch and sugar. When the starch and sugar are made, the plants have some oxygen left over. That is the oxygen which is given off by the plants. Animals use that oxygen."

"Do plants growing outside an aquarium need carbon dioxide, too?" asked Martha Lou.

"Yes," said Father. "Land animals give off carbon dioxide just as water animals do. Land plants use the carbon dioxide that goes into the air, just as water plants do."

"And land animals use oxygen that land plants give off," laughed Randy. "It's another circle."

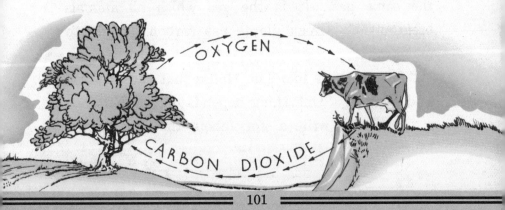

"Do we need oxygen, too?" asked Martha Lou.

"Yes, we do," said Randy. "Everybody needs oxygen. We breathe air into our lungs. Here are my lungs," Randy put his hands on his chest to show Martha Lou.

"But what happens to the air after we breathe it?" he asked his father.

"The body uses the oxygen. The oxygen is sent into every part of the body. As the body uses the oxygen, carbon dioxide is given off," said Father.

"Is it the same as the carbon dioxide the fish and other animals breathe out?" asked Martha Lou.

"Yes," said Father. "Carbon dioxide is always the same gas. It is the gas which all animals breathe out. Green plants use carbon dioxide to make food."

"This world is like The House that Jack Built," said Randy. "One thing depends on another."

"Let's each write a story about that," suggested Martha Lou.

Martha Lou's Story

This is the aquarium that Mother had.

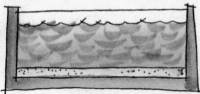

These are the plants that grew in the aquarium that Mother had.

These are the fish that used the oxygen given off by the plants that grew in the aquarium that Mother had.

These are the plants that used the carbon dioxide given off by the fish that used the oxygen given off by the plants that grew in the aquarium that Mother had.

This is the balanced aquarium that Mother had.

Randy's Story

This is the farm that Father owned.

These are the cows that lived on the farm that Father owned.

This is the fertilizer that was made by the cows that lived on the farm that Father owned.

This is the soil that was improved by the fertilizer that was made by the cows that lived on the farm that Father owned.

These are the seeds that were put in the soil that was improved by the fertilizer that was made by the cows that lived on the farm that Father owned.

These are the plants that grew from the seeds that were put in the soil that was improved by the fertilizer that was made by the cows that lived on the farm that Father owned.

These are the cows that ate the plants that grew from the seeds that were put in the soil that was improved by the fertilizer that was made by the cows that lived on the farm that Father owned.

This is the family that ate the plants that grew from the seeds that were put in the soil that was improved by the fertilizer that was made by the cows that lived on the farm that Father owned.

This is the end of my story about plants and animals, and animals and plants.

The Balance of Nature

Did you ever see scales like these?

When the sides have equal weights or no weights on them, the scales are balanced.

There is a balance in nature, too, which is not so different from the balance of scales.

The number of plants remains about the same each year. Many, many plants die each year. But many, many new plants grow each year.

The number of animals remains about the same each year. Many, many animals die each year. Many, many new animals are born each year.

If the number of animals balances the number of plants, we say there is a balance of nature.

The enemies of animals and plants help to keep this balance by killing them or crowding them out.

Sometimes man upsets the balance of nature.

Once there was a certain kind of harmful moth in the United States. This moth was killing trees. A man thought of a way to get rid of these moths. He had heard that English sparrows were the enemies of these moths. But there were no English sparrows in the United States.

This man decided to bring some English sparrows to the United States. The English sparrows were set free. They ate the harmful insects as the man expected them to do.

Was this a good experiment? Wait before you answer.

This is what happened. The English sparrows were enemies of this certain kind of insect, but the English sparrows had few enemies in the United States. They increased in number rapidly. Soon there were so many English sparrows that they drove away many of our own song birds. In order to get enough food, the English sparrows had to eat seeds that the farmers had planted for crops.

Now the English sparrows are a pest. They do great harm. People would like to get rid of the English sparrows just as they had wanted to get rid of the harmful moths.

Bones and Muscles

"I have a jig-saw puzzle," said Jimmy one morning at a meeting of the How and Why Club. "It is a bone puzzle. When it is put together, you can see where all the bones of the body are."

"Let's put it together," said Dick. "I'd like to see how my bones look."

So the children put the puzzle on a big table. They needed lots of room because the puzzle was a big one.

"Let's start with this piece," said Nancy. "This must be the head. You can see the teeth. How strong they look! I didn't know that our teeth were set in our jaw bones like that!"

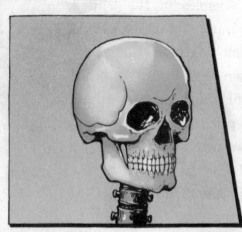

"That's why teeth are so hard to pull out," said Bob.

"Here is the rest of the neck. It fastens on right here," said Dick.

"How can there be bones in the neck?" asked Jane. "I can bend my neck easily in all directions."

"That is because of the way the bones are fastened together," said Mr. Thorne. "The bones in the head are fastened together tightly, but the bones in the neck are not. They are fastened so that you can turn your head."

"The bones in my arm aren't fastened together tightly," said Bob. "See! I can bend my arm. The bones must be hinged together."

"*Hinged* is a good word to use," said Mr. Thorne. "That's really the way they are fastened together."

"These must be the ribs," said Nancy. "See, they fit right on here."

"How many ribs can you count?" asked Mr. Thorne.

The children counted.

"I count ten on each side," Bob said.

"But there are twelve on each side," said Mr. Thorne. "The two ribs at the bottom aren't fastened in front. Can you see them?"

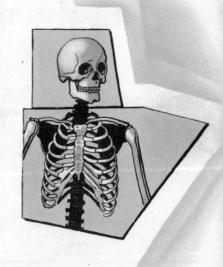

"Oh, yes," said Bob. "I didn't know those were ribs."

The children completed the puzzle. When it was all together it looked like this.

Skeleton

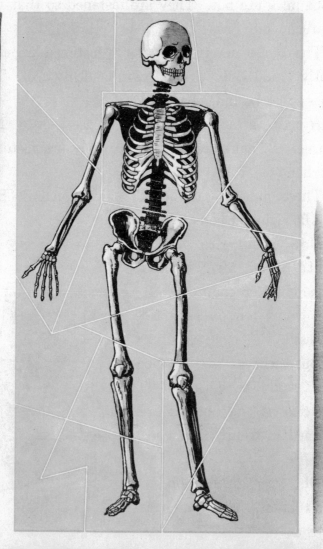

"*Skeleton* is a new word," said Dick. "All of the bones put together must be the skeleton."

"Do I have a skeleton?" asked Susan.

"Of course you do," said Jimmy. "Everybody has a skeleton."

"The skeleton is the frame for the body," said Mr. Thorne. "When we build a house, we put up a frame first. Then we build the house on the frame. Our skeletons are the frames on which our bodies are built."

"My, but there are a lot of bones in a skeleton," said Nancy as she studied the puzzle. "I wonder how many there are."

"There are more than two hundred bones in the skeleton," said Mr. Thorne. "Some of them are very small. There are three main parts to a skeleton. They are first, the head; second, the trunk; and third, the arms and legs."

"What else can we learn about a skeleton?" asked Jane.

"I think we should know its uses," said Bob. "I know that it gives the body its shape."

"Some of the bones protect the body," said Jimmy. "The ribs protect the part of the body that is inside."

"We couldn't walk or run without a skeleton," said Susan. "We couldn't sit or stand straight."

"I couldn't throw a ball," said Dick.

"I broke my arm once," said Bob. "I fell from an apple tree. The doctor put splints on both sides of my arm. He tied them firmly to my arm. When he took the splints off, the arm was well. So bones must grow together when they are broken."

"Yes," said Mr. Thorne, "that is another thing to know about bones. Can you show us on this skeleton which bone you broke?"

"Let me see," said Bob. "My arm was broken here. Then it must have been this bone." Bob put his finger on the correct bone of the skeleton.

"I have seen the bones in my feet," said Jane. "When Mother bought my new shoes, I put my feet in a machine. I could see the bones of my feet."

"That is a good way to fit shoes," said Mr. Thorne. "Shoes should be worn that are large enough to let the bones grow straight."

"There is something on the other side of this puzzle," said Bob.

This is how the other side of the puzzle looked.

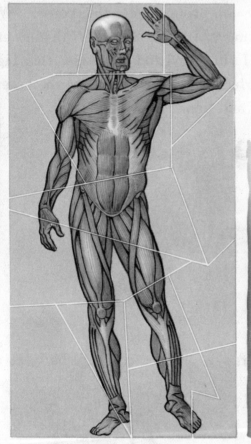

"Now the bones are all covered up," said Jimmy. "They are covered with muscles."

"It looks like a man without skin," laughed Bob.

"That's what it is," said Dick.

"What do muscles do?" asked Susan.

"Muscles move the bones," said Jimmy.

"How can they move the bones?" asked Nancy.

"They are fastened to the bones. When the muscles move, the bones move," Jimmy explained. "When I lift my hand like this, this big muscle gets shorter and bigger. It raises the lower part of my arm and hand."

"I'll draw a picture for you," he went on.

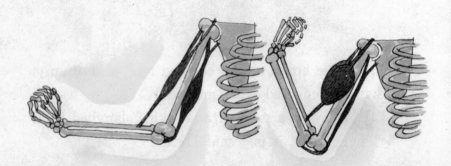

"That is good, Jimmy," said Mr. Thorne. "When the muscle gets shorter and thicker, we say it *contracts*. When it gets longer, it *relaxes*. Every movement that the body makes is caused by muscles contracting and relaxing. In your picture, when one muscle contracts, it pulls the hand up. Then that muscle relaxes and another muscle contracts and pulls the hand back to where it was. We run, jump, walk, and move by means of muscles that contract and relax."

"Then muscles must do a lot of work," said Susan.

"They must need a lot of food," said Nancy.

"My dad says that muscles need lots of exercise," said Bob. "Boys and girls who exercise their muscles by working and playing grow strong."

The children decided to make a list of things about muscles. Dick wrote the list on the board.

1. Muscles cover the bones of the skeleton.
2. Muscles move the bones.
3. Muscles make possible all movements of the body.
4. Muscles need food.
5. Muscles get longer as we grow.
6. Muscles get stronger with exercise.

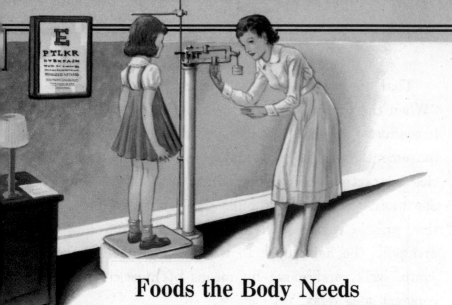

Foods the Body Needs

Experimenting with Foods

"The nurse told me that I must gain ten pounds," said Jane one day. "She told me to eat more starch, sugar, and fat. I'd like to know how I can tell what things have starch, sugar, and fat in them."

"Our How and Why Club can find that out," said Jimmy. "We learned that cornstarch and potatoes have starch in them. We learned that butter and fat meat have fat stored in them. We could test other foods, too."

"And let's find out what it is in food that makes it good for us," said Nancy. "Mother is always saying 'This is good for you,' or 'This isn't good for you.' Why does she say those things? I'd like to know."

The children brought many different things to test. During their club meeting they experimented with foods they had brought.

"Iodine is a test for starch," Jimmy reminded the children.

"Let's begin," spoke out Dick.

"Remember, Dick, we must work carefully," warned Susan. "Let's have Jane experiment first. She is the one who needs to know the most about starch."

Jane had brought some bread. She put some iodine on it. The spot where the iodine was put on the bread turned dark blue.

"Bread has starch in it," cried Jane.

"Let's put all the things with starch in them on this table," said Nancy. "Then we'll have them all together."

"I brought some green peas," said Susan. "Let me try them. They are cooked." Only a little blue showed on the peas when iodine was put on them.

"Green peas don't have much starch in them," said Dick. "Let's put the things without much starch on this other table. Then we will have all things without much starch together."

"I brought a cracker," continued Dick. "Want me to test it?"

"Yes!" said Bob.

The spot on the cracker turned dark blue as soon as the iodine touched it.

"Crackers must have a lot of starch in them," said Nancy. "Put the cracker on the table with the bread, and watch my experiment.

"I brought some flour. I think it has starch in it, but I want to be sure."

As soon as the iodine touched the flour, a blue spot was formed.

"Flour must have a lot of starch," said Nancy as she put the flour with the bread and the cracker.

"What did you bring, Bob?" asked Jane.

"I have a piece of apple and some nuts," he said.

Bob dropped some iodine on the apple. No blue spot was formed. "This apple does not have starch in it," he said.

Then he tried a nut. There was no change of color. "The nut doesn't have starch in it," he said. "It belongs on the table with the green peas."

"I want to test my oatmeal," said Susan. "It has been cooked. When the iodine was put on the oatmeal, a blue spot immediately appeared. "Cooked oatmeal must have starch in it," said Susan, as she put it on the table with the starchy foods.

"I have some cereals, too," said Jimmy. "They are the kind we eat without cooking. One is made from wheat and one is made from corn." He put some iodine on each of them. Blue color immediately appeared.

"Oh! Cereals have starch in them!" cried the children.

"Cereals should be good for you to eat, Jane," said Susan.

"I like cereals," said Jane. "I think I shall eat some kind of cereal every morning. Bread should be good for me, too."

"Mr. Thorne, did you bring something to test?" asked Nancy.

"Yes, I soaked some wheat and corn kernels last night. I thought you might be interested to see if the seed has starch stored in it. Jimmy, cut open a kernel of corn and put some iodine on it," said Mr. Thorne.

When the corn kernel was cut open, it looked like this.

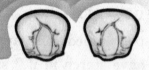

When Jimmy put some iodine on the cut part, the kernel looked like this.

"Look!" exclaimed Jimmy. "Not all of the kernel is blue. Most of it is blue but part of it isn't."

"Starch is stored in almost all of a corn kernel," Mr. Thorne told the children. "But a little part of each kernel does not store starch. That part is 'the little plant.' It is sometimes called the germ of the seed."

"Does the wheat kernel have a little plant too?" asked Dick. "Let's test it."

"The wheat kernel contains starch, too," said Bob as soon as Jimmy dropped some iodine on it. "And see! It has a little plant in it, too. The little plant didn't turn blue as the rest of the kernel did."

"Much of our flour is made from wheat," put in Jane. "It must be made from the starchy part of wheat."

"That's right, Jane," said Mr. Thorne. "Flour is made from the starchy part of wheat. What do you think is made from the starchy part of corn?"

"Cornstarch," said Nancy. "We experimented with cornstarch last fall."

"Is anything made from the germs of the seeds?" asked Bob.

"Yes," answered Mr. Thorne. "The germ of corn contains fat. Corn oil is made from it. Many things are made from corn oil. Soap is one of them. Some cooking oil is made from corn oil, also. Sometimes the whole grains of both corn and wheat are used for breakfast foods and for bread."

"I think the secretary should make a list of the things we have tested that have starch in them," said Jimmy.

Nancy wrote two lists on the blackboard. In one list she put the things that contain much starch. In the other list she put the things that do not contain much starch.

These things contain much starch:

bread	cereals
crackers	cornstarch
flour	potatoes
oatmeal	

These things do not contain much starch:

green peas	salt
apples	carrots
nuts	beets

"Now I know some things that contain starch," said Jane. "What else should I eat?"

"You should eat well-balanced meals," said Mr. Thorne. "Your body needs starch but it needs other foods, too. You see, your food does certain things for you all of the time. Food gives heat to keep you warm. Food furnishes energy. Energy makes you want to do things. Food makes you fat. The right amount of fat helps make you healthy. Your body uses food to make bone and blood and muscle. Food keeps you strong. Every day you use a great deal of energy. You have to eat food in order to supply your body with more energy."

"Our bodies must be something like furnaces," said Jimmy. "We have to shovel in coal to keep the fire burning!"

"That's right," said Mr. Thorne. "Starch and sugar give you energy. They help you gain weight, too. Fat also gives you energy. Can you name something that contains fat?"

"Butter," said Dick.

"Cream," said Susan.

"Fat meat," said Bob.

"Peanuts," said Jimmy.

"Walnuts," said Jane.

"I remember how to test for fat," said Nancy. "Fat makes grease spots on blotting paper. I will put a list on the blackboard of things that contain fat."

Some things that have fat in them:

butter	fat meat
cream	nuts

"We need other things besides energy," continued Mr. Thorne. "Remember, we need food that can be used to make muscle. That food is called *protein*. There is protein in the white of an egg. There is protein in beans, too."

"Oh, I thought beans had starch in them," said Susan.

"We'll experiment to find out," said Mr. Thorne. "I soaked some bean seeds last night, when I soaked the corn and wheat kernels. Try this bean, Susan."

Susan cut the bean open and put some iodine on it. Only part of the bean contained starch.

"What other food did you say, Thorne?" asked Bob.

"Beans contain protein. They help make musc said Mr. Thorne. "Lean meat has protein in it There is protein in milk. There is protein in fish, too. Proteins help make muscle and give you strength."

"How can we experiment to find out if a food is protein?" asked Nancy.

"We would have to use chemicals that we do not have here in school," said Mr. Thorne. "For the present, you must take the word of scientists who have done the experiments. I will tell you some of the things that have protein in them."

"I think the secretary should write the names on the board," said Susan.

Mr. Thorne gave Nancy this list. Nancy wrote the list on the board.

Some protein foods:

dried beans	milk
eggs	cheese
lean meat	fish
soy beans	peanuts
cereals	dried peas

"What foods make bone?" asked Jane.

"Eggs, milk, cabbage, lettuce, and spinach help make bone," Mr. Thorne replied. "These contain calcium. Calcium is a mineral. It is a good bone food. Bones need food, just as any other part of the body does. Calcium makes bones strong. Things that contain calcium help make bones grow larger. That is why you should have some calcium every day."

"Do minerals help make blood, too?" asked Nancy.

"Yes, they do," said Mr. Thorne. "Iron is one of the minerals that help make blood. Iron and calcium and other minerals are just as necessary as starches and fats and proteins. Green vegetables contain minerals."

"My sister had to eat liver to help her make blood," said Bob. "Does liver contain minerals?"

"Yes, liver has iron in it," said Mr. Thorne. "Milk contains minerals, too."

The children asked Nancy to write the list of some mineral foods. This was her list:

Some mineral foods:

cereals	cabbage	celery	molasses
whole grain bread	lettuce	liver	dried fruits
	spinach	milk	eggs

"Milk is on two of our lists," said Bob. "Milk contains protein and it contains minerals, too. That must be why milk is good for us."

"Milk contains fat, too," said Nancy. "Cream comes from milk, and cream contains fat."

"Milk contains some sugar, too," said Mr. Thorne. "Milk contains about all the foods the body needs."

"I think we should remember the kinds of food the body needs," said Nancy. "We need to help our bodies make energy, muscle, bone, and blood. Let's see if we remember the five kinds of food that make these things."

Each child wrote:

1. Starch
2. Sugar
3. Fat
4. Protein
5. Minerals

"Starch, sugar, and fat help me gain weight," said Jane. "They give me energy, too."

"But you mustn't forget protein and minerals," reminded Nancy. "You must eat meals that help make muscles, bones, and blood."

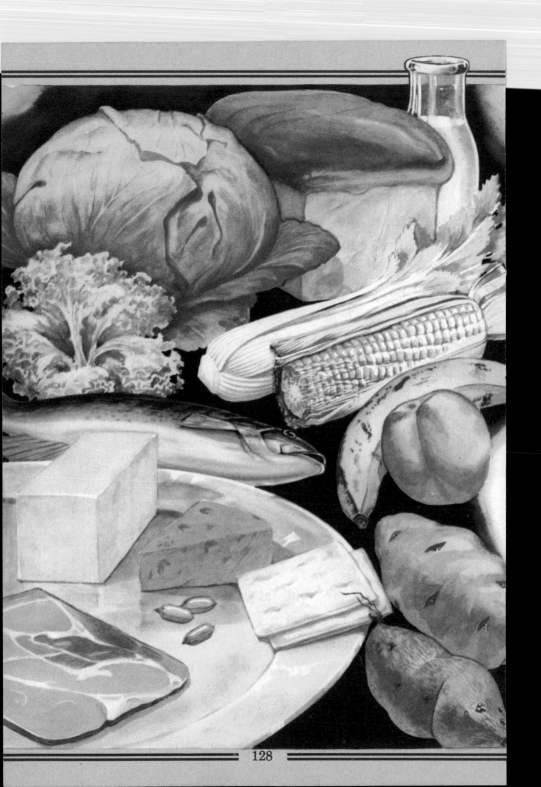

A Game About Foods

The children played a game. They found pictures of foods. Then they took turns telling whether the foods contained starch or sugar or fat or protein or minerals.

These are some of the pictures they found.

Can you pick out three foods that contain starch?

Can you pick out three foods that contain sugar?

Can you pick out three foods that contain fat?

Can you pick out five foods that contain protein?

What three foods contain minerals?

What food have you eaten today that contains starch?

What food have you eaten today that contains fat?

What food have you eaten today that contains protein?

What food have you eaten today that contains minerals?

Do you eat well-balanced meals?

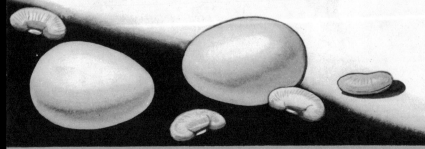

How Foods Are Used in the Body

Foods That Are Easily Dissolved

"We have found out which foods have starch in them, which ones have sugar, which ones have fat, and which ones have protein," Mr. Thorne said one day. "That is only half the story. Jimmy, does your mother ever tell you to eat more slowly?"

"Yes," said Jimmy. "She says I swallow my food whole."

"Why should you eat more slowly?" asked Mr. Thorne.

"You'll choke if you don't," said Susan.

The children laughed.

"There is another reason," said Mr. Thorne. "We will do an experiment to see what happens to food when we chew it. Jimmy, will you pass these crackers?"

"Let's all start chewing a piece of cracker at the same time," Mr. Thorne suggested. "See who can chew it the longest without swallowing."

The room was very quiet for about three minutes.

"Oh, I swallowed mine," cried Nancy. Mr. Thorne gave her another cracker. At the end of five minutes everyone was trying not to swallow. Mr. Thorne handed each child a test tube.

"Put your chewed cracker into the test tube," he said.

"Mine is almost all gone," said Bob.

"What happened to it?" asked Mr. Thorne.

"It got wet and soft," said Bob.

"Mine got sweet," said Jane.

"So did mine," said Jimmy.

"What is a cracker made of?" asked Mr. Thorne.

"It has flour in it," said Susan.

"It is salty," said Dick.

"It has starch in it," said Jane. "We tested it with iodine."

"Flour has starch in it," said Bob.

"You are all correct," said Mr. Thorne. "When you chewed the cracker something happened to the starch. Part of it changed to sugar."

"Was that a chemical change?" asked Bob.

"Yes," said Mr. Thorne. "You have a juice in your mouth called *saliva*. Saliva causes some of the starch to change to sugar."

"Why does that do any good?" asked Bob.

"We can do another experiment to help answer your question," said Mr. Thorne. "Will you get some starch and sugar from the storeroom, Jimmy? We'll need a funnel and some filter paper, also." Jimmy brought the materials from the storeroom.

"Will you taste a little of the sugar?" Mr. Thorne asked Jane. Jane put a little sugar in her mouth.

"It's sweet," she said, "and it dissolved.'

"Now taste a little starch," Mr. Thorne said.

"I don't like it," said Jane.

"Does it dissolve?" asked Mr. Thorne.

"I don't think so," said Jane.

"We put sugar in water one time to see if it dissolved," said Jimmy. "Let's try some starch."

Jimmy put some starch in water and stirred it. The water looked white. "Sugar dissolves but starch doesn't," he said.

"Perhaps some of the starch dissolved," said Jane.

"Things that are dissolved in water will go through this filter paper," said Mr. Thorne. "Things that are not dissolved will stay on the paper. Put a piece of filter paper in the funnel, Jimmy. Pour the sugar water through the paper. Jane may taste the water that comes through the paper," said Mr. Thorne.

"The water is sweet," said Jane. "The sugar must stay in the water as it goes through the paper."

"Yes, it shows that sugar dissolves in water. Jimmy, would you like to wash the funnel and put a

clean piece of filter paper in it?" Jimmy did as Mr. Thorne asked.

"Now pour the starch and water into the funnel," Mr. Thorne said.

Jimmy poured the starch and water into the funnel.

"The water that comes through the paper is clear," cried Jane. "There is no starch in it."

"We should test it before we decide," said Nancy. "We couldn't see the sugar in the water either."

The children watched while Bob put a drop of iodine into the clear water. It did not turn blue.

"There," said Jane. "The starch did not go through the filter paper. It did not dissolve."

"Sugar dissolves in water and starch doesn't," said Mr. Thorne. "Before your body can use food it has to dissolve," he went on. "The saliva in your mouth changes some of the starch to sugar. Then your body can use it."

"That's the reason Mother says to chew my food," said Jimmy.

"Would the starch dissolve if it were cooked?" asked Nancy.

"Let's try it," said Jane. They cooked the starch and filtered it. They tested the water that went through the filter paper. The test showed that some of the starch had gone through the paper.

"It is better to cook starchy foods," said Mr. Thorne. "Then the body can use starch more easily."

"Will you please tell us about digestion tomorrow?" asked Jane. Mr. Thorne said that he would.

Mr. Thorne's Story of Digestion

Food must be digested before it can be used by the body. We do not say food is dissolved by the body. We say, instead, that it is digested. Digestion means changing food so that it can be used by the body.

Digestion in your body starts in your mouth. You chew your food. You mix it with saliva. Saliva changes starch to sugar. This is a chemical change.

You swallow your food. It is soft now. It travels from your mouth into a tube.

From the tube, the food goes into your stomach. Your stomach churns the soft food. There are juices in your stomach. The juices make the food still softer. They change the food still more. Your stomach juices help digestion, just as saliva does.

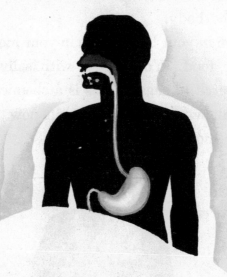

Then the food goes into your small intestine. Other juices soften the food and change it some more. The food is not solid now. It is almost as thin as water. It is almost all digested. Food must be digested before your body can use it. The digested food can go through the walls of the small intestine. It goes into your blood. The blood carries the food to all parts of your body.

Not all of the food digests. The part that is left is called *waste*. The waste travels from the small intestine into your large intestine.

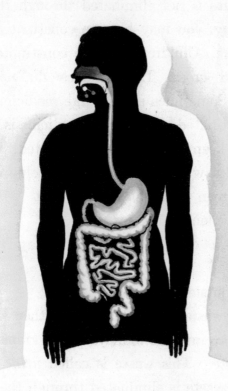

The waste must be eliminated. *To eliminate* means to get rid of. Your body must get rid of the waste. The large intestine has very strong muscles. These muscles help force the waste out of the body.

If you wish to keep well, you should see that waste is eliminated through the large intestine every day.

If waste is not eliminated through the intestines every day, you may become constipated. That is a bad thing. Children who are constipated are often sick and cross. Their bodies do not eliminate waste. Sometimes people take medicine when they are constipated. But taking medicine is not the best way to keep from being constipated. Would you like to know how to keep from being constipated?

Eat green vegetables every day.

Drink plenty of water.

Have a certain time every day to eliminate waste.

Play outside every day.

Some waste is eliminated in other ways. Some waste goes into the kidneys. The kidneys eliminate this waste. This waste is called *urine*.

Some waste is eliminated through the skin. This waste is called *sweat*.

The body eliminates waste in these ways:

1. Through the large intestine.
2. Through the kidneys.
3. Through the skin.

Questions and Answers

After Mr. Thorne had told the children these interesting things about their bodies, he gave each of them a sheet of paper. These questions were written on each sheet.

1. What juice in your mouth changes starch to sugar?
2. By what process in the body is food changed so that it can be used in the body?
3. What waste does your skin eliminate?
4. What waste do your kidneys eliminate?
5. From the mouth food goes through a tube, into your ——
6. If your intestines do not eliminate waste properly, you may become ——
7. The digested food goes through the walls of your —— in getting to the blood.

Then Mr. Thorne gave each child seven cards. The cards had these words on them:

constipated   saliva   sweat   urine
stomach   intestines   digestion

How did the children match the questions and the cards?

More Experiments with Food

The How and Why Club tried experiments every day. These are some that they tried.

1.

They boiled some whole kernels of corn for a few minutes.

They tested the water for starch.

They boiled some cracked kernels of corn for a few minutes.

They tested the water for starch.

They learned that:

1. The whole kernel of corn has an outside covering that keeps water from entering the kernel quickly.

2. The cracked grain of corn cooks much more quickly than the whole kernel.

2.

They looked at wheat kernels.

They looked at corn kernels.

They learned that:

1. Wheat kernels are smaller than corn kernels.

2. Corn kernels have the harder covering.

3.

They heated corn kernels to make them dry.

They ground the kernels between stones as the Indians used to do.

They tasted the meal that they had made.

They tested it for starch.

They learned that:

1. Corn meal made as the Indians used to make it has starch in it.

2. It tastes like parched corn.

4.

They chewed some kernels of wheat.

They chewed some kernels of corn.

The wheat became sticky.

The corn did not become sticky.

They learned that:

1. Wheat has *gluten* in it.

2. Gluten makes wheat sticky.

5.

They put one tablespoonful of wheat flour in cheesecloth.

They put one tablespoonful of cornstarch in cheesecloth.

They made the cheesecloth into little bags. They fastened each bag with string.

They washed each bag in water until the water was clear.

The bag with the cornstarch soon had nothing left in it.

The bag with the wheat flour had something sticky and yellow left in it.

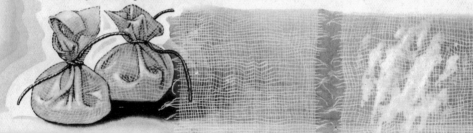

They learned that:

1. The sticky yellow substance was gluten.

2. Gluten makes it possible for us to make raised breads and cakes from wheat flour.

3. Cornstarch has no gluten. It can not be used for making raised breads and cakes.

6.

They stirred a little water into some flour.

They put some yeast in the flour and water.

They put the dough in a warm place.

Big bubbles came in the dough.

The bubbles made the dough rise.

They learned that:

1. Yeast helps to raise breads that are made from wheat flour.

2. Yeast is a little plant.

3. It grows and gives off a gas.

4. The gas makes bubbles in the bread.

5. It raises the bread.

6. The gluten in the flour hardens when it bakes and holds the loaf of bread in shape.

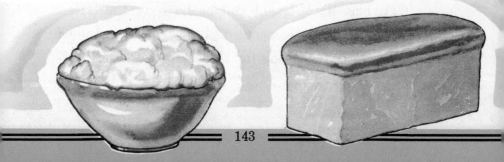

Jack Finds Some Fossils

Jack had to take a letter to Bill, the sheep herder. Bill lived in a sheep wagon in the mountains. He looked after the sheep that grazed on the mountain sides. When the sheep had eaten the grass from one place, Bill moved his wagon and drove his sheep to another place. Then he let the sheep graze in the new place.

Jack did not know just where he would find Bill. He rode Rat Tail along the mountain trails until he saw sheep grazing. Then he knew that Bill was somewhere near. Soon he saw Bill's sheep wagon near a stream of water.

"Hi, Bill," Jack shouted.

Bill came to the door of his wagon and waved.

"Hi, yourself, Jack. Glad to see you."

Jack jumped off Rat Tail and ran to the wagon. He handed Bill the letter.

"Here's a letter for you, Bill," he said. "It came by air mail. Dad thought it might be important."

"Thanks, Jack," said Bill as he took the letter. "It's good to see someone again. I haven't talked to anyone but my dog for three weeks. I get lonesome up here sometimes."

While Bill was reading his letter, Jack walked toward a stream that trickled down the mountain side. He noticed some unusual looking tracks in a rock and knelt down to look at them.

"What queer looking tracks! They're in the rock. What kind are they, Bill?" he asked, as Bill walked toward him.

"They *are* peculiar," answered Bill. "They look as if some animal had made them. But no animal *I* know anything about could make tracks that large."

"I guess I'll ask Cowboy Hal to come up," said Jack. "Maybe he can tell us what kind of animal made them."

The next day Cowboy Hal came to Bill's camp with Jack. When he saw the tracks in the rock, he exclaimed, "Say Jack! Those are fossils! Perfect fossils! The best I ever saw!"

"What's a fossil!" asked Jack.

"A fossil may be a print of an animal or a plant that is left in a rock," Cowboy Hal explained. "It may even be the remains of an animal or plant that lived long ago. It may be large or small. Fossils that have been found seem to show that a long time ago some huge animals lived on the earth. They were larger than any animals living today. But finally they all died. Their skeletons were covered with mud and all that remains today is the print of their skeletons or tracks that were left when the mud hardened. You have found fossil footprints of one of those ancient animals. We'll see if we can find out about those animals in your new reference books."

They rode back to the ranch and looked in Jack's new books. There were many pictures of the ancient animals.

"Whew! What enormous fellows they were!" cried Jack. "They must have been lots larger than elephants. And look at their names! The names are almost as big as the animals. Cowboy Hal, how do you say this name?"

Cowboy Hal told him how to say *di-no-saur*.

"There were many kinds of dinosaurs," said Cowboy Hal, "just as there are now many kinds of birds and many kinds of fish. Here is a big fellow! This one is called a *Bron-to-saur-us*. It means 'thunder lizard.'"

"A Brontosaurus was so large," continued Cowboy Hal, "it could almost shake the ground when it moved. Can you imagine an animal seventy feet long, Jack? That's longer than our barn. And an animal seventy feet long must have weighed several tons!"

Jack laughed. "I'd like to see an animal as big as our barn! I don't see how it could even move!"

"As a matter of fact, dinosaurs couldn't move very fast," said Cowboy Hal. "They were the most stupid creatures you can imagine. At least, we think they were stupid. You see, no man ever saw one of these creatures."

"Then how do we know they lived and what they looked like?" asked Jack.

"That's an interesting story," said Cowboy Hal. "When men first found tracks like those you found, they didn't know what animals had made them.

They found footprints, the prints of bones, and sometimes whole bones. At first people were not so curious about the prints. Finally there were some men who became very much interested in them. The prints told stories of ancient life. They dug into the ground and uncovered more prints. The men poured wax into the prints and when the wax was cold, they lifted it out. They found that the wax had been molded in the shape of bones. They kept on doing this until they had wax models of many of the bones and teeth of animals. Then they put them together. It was hard work and took a great deal of patience. But when all the models were put together, they looked like the skeleton of a huge animal. Here is a picture of such a skeleton. From this and similar skeletons the pictures of dinosaurs in your books have been drawn."

"I wonder what kind of animal made the tracks I found," said Jack. "None of these books tell me."

Jack sent to the library in town for some books about animals that lived long ago. The books had interesting pictures in them. They answered many of Jack's questions. They did not tell him which animal made the footprints.

"The men who put the skeletons together had to imagine how the animals looked," Jack told Cowboy Hal. "Those men had to know a great deal about animals."

"Yes, they knew that bones can not move without muscles to make them move," said Cowboy Hal, "so they put in models of muscles where muscles should be. They also knew that every animal has a covering to protect the muscles and bones. The men then imagined the kind of skin the big animals had. Usually they could tell from the bones whether the animals were fish or birds or land animals. Sometimes they had to guess."

"I think I'll do some guessing about my fossils," said Jack. "I'll make up a story about them."

"Why not write a letter to a man who knows a great deal about fossils?" suggested Cowboy Hal.

"Perhaps he could tell you something about the foot-prints you found."

This is the letter that Jack wrote. He sent it to a man who worked in a museum. Fossils of ancient animals were kept in the museum.

Dear Sir:

I found some fossils. They look like this:

Can you tell me what kind of animal of long ago made them?

Yours truly,
Jack Hill

Jack was very much excited when he received this answer. He read it to Cowboy Hal.

Dear Jack,

Your letter concerning the fossils sounds very interesting. You may have found the prints of a rare animal. May I come to your ranch and look around for myself? Then I can tell you about your fossils and perhaps I can find some more.

Sincerely yours,
Joseph E. Peters

"He'll come to our ranch!" cried Jack. "Isn't that great?"

Jack wrote Mr. Peters a letter immediately and invited him to come to the ranch. A week later Cowboy Hal and Jack rode to town to meet the train. When Mr. Peters stepped off the train, Jack said, "How do you do, Mr. Peters. I'm Jack Hill. I'm glad you came."

"Thank you, Jack," said Mr. Peters as he took Jack's hand. "We'll have some fun exploring, I'm sure. We're partners right now. I hope we find a lot of fossils."

Early the next morning, Jack, Cowboy Hal, and Mr. Peters rode off to Bill's camp.

As soon as Mr. Peters saw Jack's fossils he said, "Those are some of the best fossils I have ever seen. I think they are the footprints of a dinosaur. Which dinosaur, I'm not sure. But I'll find out. Perhaps I can find more fossils. Then I can build a model of the animal as it used to be.

"This is a fossil of a tooth," he said, after he began exploring.

"And this is a fossil of part of the backbone.

"These prints look as if only one animal had made them. If that is so, we are very lucky. Often we find fossils of many animals in the same place. Then it is hard to separate the fossils and build the model of just one animal. This animal may have come here for water and died at this spot. Its skeleton was covered with mud. For ages and ages it has remained here in this same place. The prints of its bones were left in the mud. The mud finally turned into rock. The rock was covered with dirt. Finally water washed the dirt away from the rock and now we can see the fossils.

"There were several kinds of dinosaurs," he explained. "One dinosaur was a plant eater. It was a very curious animal. It had two rows of large plates along its back. Its tail was probably used as a weapon against its enemies.

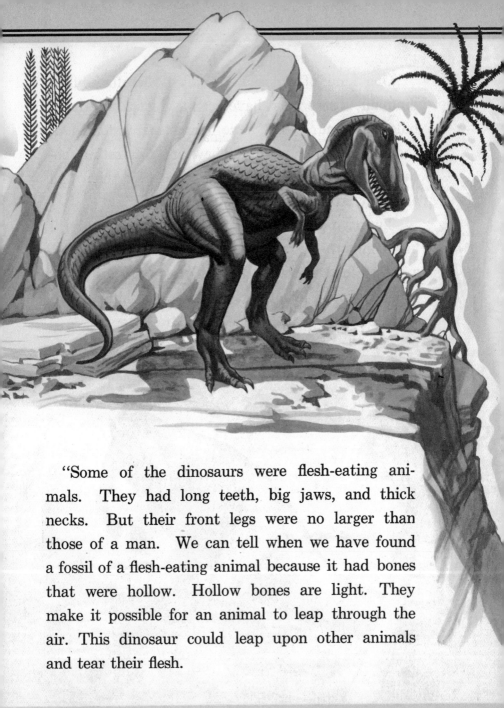

"Some of the dinosaurs were flesh-eating animals. They had long teeth, big jaws, and thick necks. But their front legs were no larger than those of a man. We can tell when we have found a fossil of a flesh-eating animal because it had bones that were hollow. Hollow bones are light. They make it possible for an animal to leap through the air. This dinosaur could leap upon other animals and tear their flesh.

"One kind of dinosaur is called the duck-billed dinosaur. There must have been a great many duck-billed dinosaurs. We have found many fossils of them. They ate plants. They are interesting because they had so many teeth. Some of them had as many as twenty-five hundred teeth!"

"Twenty-five hundred!" laughed Jack. "And I'll have only thirty-two when I'm grown. My! what a lot of food those teeth could take care of!"

"But what a lot of toothaches a duck-billed dinosaur could have had!" laughed Mr. Peters.

"Why aren't there dinosaurs on the earth now?" asked Jack.

"There are different ideas about that," said Mr. Peters. "Scientists believe that dinosaurs were cold-blooded animals that had to live in a wet, warm country. They think the climate of the world may have changed while the dinosaurs were living. They think the dinosaurs may have died because they could not stand the change.

"It seems also that many of the dinosaurs had poor teeth and could eat only the tenderest of plants. Some scientists think that the plant life may have changed. They think the dinosaurs may have died because they could not get enough food.

"Many scientists believe that dinosaurs could not protect themselves. Dinosaurs were big and clumsy. They could not move fast. They were so awkward they could not fight all their enemies.

"Another belief is that the dinosaurs may have been drowned by the seas which overflowed the land at one time."

"Were dinosaurs the only animals that lived long ago?" asked Jack.

"Oh, no," said Mr. Peters. "There were many other animals. We have found fossils of them."

"Fossils certainly tell interesting stories about animals," said Jack.

"Fossils tell interesting stories about plants, too," said Mr. Peters. "In many places fossils of plants have been found.

"It is certain that some plants which once grew on the earth have also disappeared. Some of them seem to have been enormous plants—much larger than any we have today. Most of them seem to have been large ferns. It is believed that these ferns grew in damp places, so close together that they looked like great forests.

"When the plants died they were covered with mud. The leaves of the plants made prints in the mud. Many, many plants were pressed together. After years and years they formed coal. We find fossils of ferns and large plants in beds of coal.

"The shells and bones of water animals were pressed together in the same way. After many, many years they formed limestone. These animals were mostly animals like snails, clams, and coral. Many such fossils may be found in limestone."

Mr. Peters worked for days and days digging in the rocks. He put wax into every print that he found. The wax hardened and came out in the shape of bones. Then he made models of every bone print he had found.

When he had finished, he said, "Jack, you found fossils of one of the largest dinosaurs known. This animal was a Brontosaurus."

"Oh!" cried Jack, "that's the name Cowboy Hal and I found in my book."

"We have not found many fossils of this animal, but from those we have found, we know that it was huge," said Mr. Peters. "We have found most of the fossils in old lake beds. These animals had no way to protect themselves except to go into lakes. Then they could get away from their enemies, the flesh-eating dinosaurs. They had long, thin necks which made it possible for them to stay in deep water. They were different from the flesh-eating dinosaurs because they walked on four feet. The flesh-eating dinosaurs walked on their two hind feet, and their two front legs were helpless. But they were all stupid creatures.

"This is the best fossil of a Brontosaurus I have ever seen," he told Jack. "When I have packed it and taken it to the museum, I'll put the bones together. I can construct the best Brontosaurus model in any museum. And you, Jack, are responsible for this fossil. You found the prints and wrote me about them. Sometime you must come to see me and I'll show you the other dinosaurs we have constructed from fossils. You have been a fine little worker, Jack. Good-bye and good luck to you."

Several months later Jack received a package from Mr. Peters. It contained a photograph of a model of the Brontosaurus as it had been put together at the museum.

"Just think!" said Jack. "I discovered this Brontosaurus when I found those fossils up at Bill's sheep camp!"

Why Does Food Spoil?

A Strange Plant

Susan came to the meeting of the How and Why Club one morning with a strange-looking piece of bread to show the children. It was black and furry. All the children wanted to see what it was.

"Did you ever see any bread that looked like this?" Susan asked.

"I have," said Nancy. "Mother showed me a piece. She showed me a piece of cake, too, that

looked black and furry. Mother said something happened to it while we were away from home for a week. She said the cake got furry because the air in the bread can was moist and warm."

"I opened a glass of strawberry jam last night and it looked just like that on the top," said Jane.

"And I found some of it the other day when I went to the cellar to get an apple," said Bob. "Three of the apples in the bottom of the basket were all fuzzy like that."

"Oh, that fuzz comes on lots of things," said Jimmy. "When my uncle took his riding boots out of the closet last summer, he found some of that stuff on one of them."

"What causes it?" asked Jane.

"Why don't we do an experiment to find out?" asked Jimmy.

"That is an excellent idea, Jimmy," answered Mr. Thorne. "Tonight when you go home, ask your mother for a small amount of apple jelly. Bring it to school and we'll do an experiment."

The next day Jimmy brought a dish of jelly to school. Mr. Thorne put some dust from the window sill on the jelly. He put it in the closet. A few days later the children looked at the jelly.

"Look! That fuzzy stuff has started to come on top of the jelly," cried Nancy.

"Not only on top," said Jimmy. "It's going all the way down into the jelly! See, it has some things that look like threads growing down. Is it a plant, Mr. Thorne?"

"Yes, Jimmy, it is a plant," said Mr. Thorne. "Those tiny threads get food from the jelly. This food makes the plant grow."

"What is the name of the plant?" asked Susan.

"We call this plant *mold*," answered Mr. Thorne. "We say food or clothing is *moldy* when this plant is growing on it."

"Yesterday mother showed me a jar of grape juice that had mold on it," said Nancy. "She told me not to drink it. It had spoiled."

"That sometimes happens to fruit that is put away in bottles or jars," said Mr. Thorne. "How did your mother make her grape juice, Nancy?"

"Mother didn't make it alone," said Nancy proudly. "I helped her. It took us a whole day."

"Tell us about it," said Mr. Thorne. "What did you do first?"

"Mother told me to wash my hands with hot water and soap. She told me that everything that touched the fruit must be perfectly clean. Then I picked the grapes off the stems, and washed them several times."

"While I was washing the grapes," Nancy continued, "Mother put all the jars and covers in a big pan and boiled them."

"Why did the jars and covers have to be boiled?" asked Susan.

"Nancy's mother boiled the jars to make them perfectly clean," answered Mr. Thorne. "There might have been some little mold plants in the jars. Boiling water kills those plants. Did your mother boil the grapes, too?"

"Yes," said Nancy. "She boiled them for a long time. Then she put the boiling juice into the hot jars. She fastened the covers quickly."

"What was all the rush about?" asked Dick.

"Mother said she had to work quickly so no tiny plants in the air could get in before the juice was cool. Mold can not live if the juice is boiling hot," said Nancy.

"If she fixed every jar the same way, I don't see why one spoiled," said Jimmy.

"The cover of that jar did not fit tightly enough to keep the air out. As the juice cooled, it took up less room. This left a space in the top of the jar.

Air came into this space because the cover was not tight. The mold plants came in with the air," said Mr. Thorne. "The juice was not hot enough to kill them. They started to grow on the grape juice. As they grew, they made the juice spoil."

Another Strange Plant

"If mold is a plant, Mr. Thorne, why doesn't it have leaves?" asked Susan the next day.

"Mold is a different kind of plant. It is not a green plant," answered Mr. Thorne. "It does not have roots. It does not have seeds, either. It can not make its own food as green plants do. The tiny, thread-like parts that you saw reaching down into the jelly absorb the food for the plant. As the mold grows, small black dots that look like pepper come on top of the plant. These are tiny cases. They contain what we call *spores*. These spores grow into new plants. When the mold has used up all the food, it dies. Then its spores are carried away in the air. When they fall on food in a warm, moist place, they may begin to grow and make the food spoil."

"Are there any other plants besides mold that make foods spoil?" asked Susan.

"Yes," said Mr. Thorne, "there are other plants that cause foods to spoil, but they are so small we can not see them."

"How can we tell that food is spoiled if we can't see anything on it?" asked Dick.

"Sometimes we can tell spoiled food by its bad odor or taste," said Mr. Thorne.

"Our dog left a piece of meat out of doors in the sun," said Bob. "The meat spoiled and smelled bad."

"I remember an experiment I did with two bottles of milk," said Dick. "The milk in one bottle spoiled before the milk in the other bottle did. It got sour. That bottle was not washed clean."

"There were tiny plants that you could not see in that bottle. When the plants started to grow, the milk soured," said Mr. Thorne. "When there are many of these tiny plants in the milk, it sours quickly."

"We sell the milk from our cows," said Dick. "We keep the cows and the barn clean. We don't let any one who is sick work around the cows. We wash all the bottles in warm soapsuds. Then we put them into boiling water."

"You are doing the right thing, Dick," said Mr. Thorne. "Milk is one of our most valuable foods if it is kept perfectly clean. People who drink milk that is not clean often get sick."

"Mother always puts our bottles of milk where it is cold," said Nancy. "She says the milk will stay sweet longer if it is in a cold place."

"That is because these tiny plants can not grow in a very cold place," said Mr. Thorne.

"Meat and butter and fruit should be kept cold, too," said Jimmy.

"And all kinds of cooked vegetables," said Jane. "My mother keeps raw vegetables and fruit in our vegetable cellar. It's cool and dry down there."

"Oh, I know now why many foods are frozen," said Bob. "That is one way to keep them from spoiling."

"That is right," said Mr. Thorne. "Many fruits and vegetables are frozen soon after they are picked. Then they are kept frozen until they are sold."

"Yes, and Mother puts the little packages right into our refrigerator and keeps them there until she is ready to cook them," said Nancy. "That is a good way to keep things fresh."

"Raw vegetables and fresh fruits keep well in a clean vegetable cellar. But there are many foods that have to be kept much colder than they would be in a cellar. We keep them in a refrigerator. The temperature of the air in refrigerators is about 50.

The temperature is so cold that the tiny plants in our food can't grow. Milk, butter, and meat are foods that should be kept in a refrigerator."

"The cold air in a refrigerator keeps the tiny plants from growing, but it does not kill them," said Mr. Thorne. "When the food gets warm the tiny plants start to grow."

"Do these tiny plants have a name?" asked Nancy.

"Yes," answered Mr. Thorne. "They are called *bacteria*. Bacteria live in many places. They live in water, in the soil, in some kinds of food, in our clothing, and in our bodies. There are different kinds of bacteria. Some bacteria cause foods to spoil."

"If we can't see bacteria, how do we know that there are different kinds?" asked Jimmy.

"That is a good question, Jimmy," said Mr. Thorne. "Do you remember how you learned about the different shapes of snowflakes and frost crystals? And do you remember seeing the patterns of sugar and salt crystals?"

"Oh, yes," said Jimmy. "We looked at the snowflakes and the other crystals through a reading glass. The reading glass made them look larger and we could see them better."

"Bacteria have to be made to look larger before we can see them," explained Mr. Thorne. "But an ordinary reading glass does not make them look large enough. We can not see bacteria even through a reading glass.

"When scientists want to study these tiny plants they use an instrument which is like a reading glass, but which is much more powerful. It makes the plants look a great deal larger. The instrument is called a *microscope*. We can see many things with a microscope that are too small for us to see without it."

"What does a microscope look like?" asked Nancy.

"Here is a microscope," said Mr. Thorne as he brought one from the cupboard.

"May we look through it, Mr. Thorne?" asked Nancy. "Maybe we can see some bacteria."

"Of course you may look through the microscope," said Mr. Thorne. "I'll fix it for you."

All the children looked through the microscope. They looked at different things. Pictures of some of the things they saw are shown on page 175.

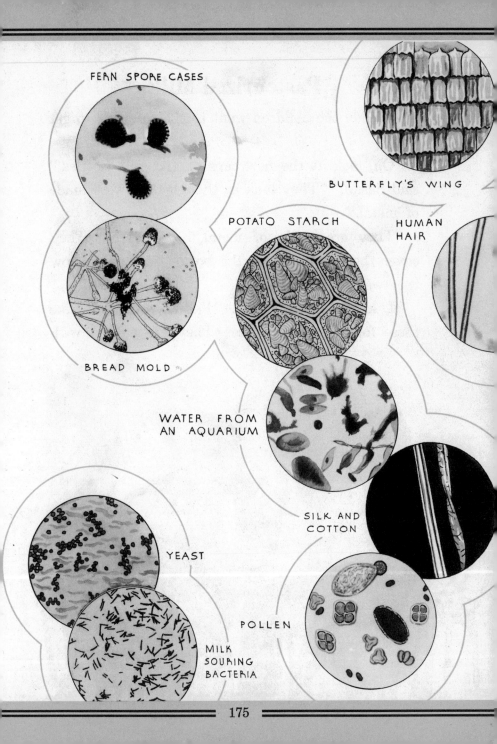

FERN SPORE CASES

BUTTERFLY'S WING

POTATO STARCH

HUMAN HAIR

BREAD MOLD

WATER FROM AN AQUARIUM

SILK AND COTTON

YEAST

POLLEN

MILK SOURING BACTERIA

Pasteurized Milk

At noon the children went to the cafeteria to get lunch.

"Oh, look at the new caps on the milk bottles," said Susan. "They look as though they were made of metal."

"They *are* made of metal," said Bob. "They cover the whole top of the bottle. I wonder how they were put on."

"I know," said Dick. "Father uses tops like these for his milk bottles. They are put on with

a machine. After the bottles have been washed, nobody touches them until they have been filled with milk and the caps put on. Father says it is the sanitary way to bottle milk."

"When the cap is over the edge of the bottle, the edge stays clean," said Jimmy. "When the milk is poured out, no dirt comes off the edge of the bottle."

"These metal caps have printing on them," said Nancy. "Look at this big name in the middle of the cap."

"That word *Pasteurized* has to be printed on every cap," said Dick. "In this town it is against the law to sell milk that hasn't been Pasteurized."

"What does 'Pasteurized' mean?" asked Nancy.

"Pasteurized milk is milk that has been heated and then cooled quickly," explained Dick. "The heat kills many bacteria in the milk. Milk that hasn't been Pasteurized is called *raw* milk."

"That's why mother boiled her grapes when she made grape juice," said Nancy. "Boiling killed the bacteria."

"But milk isn't boiled when it is Pasteurized," said Dick. "It isn't heated to such a high temperature. It is heated to a temperature of 150, and kept at that temperature for at least half an hour. Then it is cooled quickly and put into bottles."

"Pasteurized milk stays sweet longer than raw milk," added Dick.

"I know why that is," said Bob. "Some bacteria cause milk to sour. Some bacteria cause disease. When the bacteria in the milk have been killed, there isn't so much danger of our getting sick when we drink the milk."

"Why do we call it 'Pasteurized' milk?" asked Susan. "Why don't we just call it heated milk?"

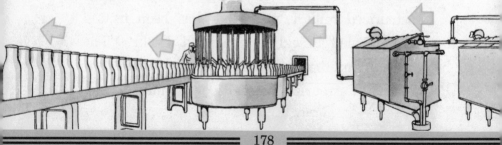

"I think the word 'Pasteurized' comes from a man's name," said Dick, "but I'm not sure. Let's ask Mr. Thorne. He will tell us."

"Mr. Thorne, does the word 'Pasteurized' come from a man's name?" asked Bob when the children were back in their schoolroom.

"Yes," said Mr. Thorne. "It comes from the name of Louis Pasteur, who was a great scientist. Pasteur discovered the importance of bacteria to man. He not only discovered the importance of bacteria, but he taught other men how to prevent sickness caused by bacteria."

"I wish you would tell us more about him, Mr. Thorne," said Jimmy.

"I'll be glad to," said Mr. Thorne. "And I will show you a picture of him. Perhaps you can find pictures of him, too, to bring to school."

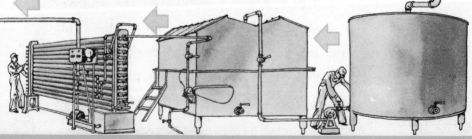

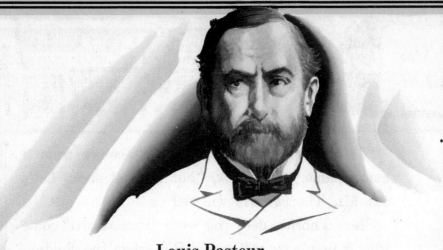

Louis Pasteur

The next day Mr. Thorne told the children some interesting things about Louis Pasteur.

"Louis Pasteur lived in France about a hundred years ago," he said. "One of the first and most exciting experiments he did was to find out where bacteria come from. He invented a flask with a long curved neck. A flask is a thin glass bottle. Scientists use flasks in experiments.

"He filled the flask with broth that would spoil quickly if bacteria got into it. Then he boiled the broth in the flask. While the steam was still coming out of the end of the tube, he heated the end and closed the opening. After it had cooled, he broke the end and let air rush into the flask. The dust in the air stayed in the curve of the tube and did not get to the broth. The broth did not spoil.

"Then Pasteur shook the flask. The broth touched some of the dust in the tube. The broth spoiled. Pasteur then thought that bacteria lived in dusty air.

"He wanted to be sure of his experiment. He made many more flasks with long curved necks. He filled them with broth. He opened some of them in dark cellars where there was no dust. Others he opened out on country roads and in school yards. Still others he took to the tops of snow-covered mountains and opened them where there was no dust."

"Experiments like that must have taken a long time," said Jimmy.

"They did," said Mr. Thorne. "Pasteur worked for several years before he was sure that bacteria were carried by dust in the air."

"What did he do then?" asked Susan.

"That is a long story," said Mr. Thorne. "Pasteur taught doctors that some bacteria cause disease. The doctors wouldn't believe him at first. He finally proved to the doctors that when they operated on patients, bacteria could get into open cuts."

"Didn't the doctors know that?" asked Jimmy.

"No," said Mr. Thorne, "nobody knew it until Pasteur discovered it. He taught the doctors how to make instruments and bandages so clean that no bacteria remained on them. He taught them to use clean instruments and clean bandages when they operated on patients. His teaching has saved the lives of many, many people."

"We used to live near the Pasteur Institute in Chicago," said Jane. "Did that institute get its name from Louis Pasteur?"

"Yes, it did," said Mr. Thorne. "That institute was named for Louis Pasteur. The scientists and doctors who work in the Pasteur Institute are continuing the work that Pasteur started. Among other things, they cure people of the disease that comes from the bite of mad dogs."

"That's hydrophobia, isn't it?" asked Jimmy.

"Yes," said Mr. Thorne. "Louis Pasteur did experiments with many, many diseases among different kinds of animals. He found cures for diseases in chickens, in sheep, in silk worms. He saved the lives of a great many farm animals."

"Now I know why our milk is called Pasteurized milk," said Susan. "Louis Pasteur learned how important it is to kill bacteria. Pasteurizing kills harmful bacteria in milk."

Winter's Picture Book

Outside, the snow was falling in big soft flakes. Inside, the room was cozy and warm. Jane sat curled up in a big chair near the fireplace. It was one of the things she liked most about a snowy Sunday afternoon. She could sit in the warm living room and read. She liked to be comfortable when it was cold outside. It gave her a good feeling to see the snow piling on the window sill and then to look at the firelight on the wall.

Jane looked up from her story as her father came into the room. "What does 'winter's picture book' mean, Dad?" she asked.

Dad looked toward the window. "I think that might be part of it there," he said. "Why do you ask?"

"In this book there is a poem which says:

Today I went a-tracking game
Down by the little brook,
It wasn't deer or bear I sought.
I didn't even look
For elephant or tiger prints
Upon the snow. I thought
That I might find a story there
From winter's picture book. "

"Oh," laughed Dad, "I've seen stories in the snow. Would you like to see some?"

"You're joking," said Jane.

"Perhaps a little bit," answered Dad. "But if it stops snowing tonight, I may be able to show you a few stories before you go to school in the morning."

The next morning Jane was up before Mother called. She dressed quickly and ran downstairs. Dad was waiting for her in the living room. It had stopped snowing. The lawn was smooth and white.

"Doesn't it look like a page in a book?" asked Dad, when Jane joined him at the living room window.

"Yes, but there isn't any picture," said Jane.

"Put on your coat and overshoes and let's go out toward the garden," suggested Dad. "Breakfast isn't ready yet."

"The snow isn't very deep," said Jane as they went down the walk.

"Something has been in the garden since it stopped snowing," said Dad.

"How do you know?" asked Jane.

Dad pointed to some tiny tracks that went across the path and out toward the vegetable garden. They were so small that Jane didn't see them at first.

"Let's follow them," said Jane.

They walked along a little way. The tracks stopped above a frozen turnip top. There was a hole down into the turnip.

"I wonder what animal made these tracks?" said Jane.

"I think it was a mouse," said Dad. "There are wild mice that make their nests in holes under stones and in other places away from the storm. But they have to get food. This mouse has found the turnips which I didn't dig last autumn. The mice don't often come out during the day. They wait until night. After it stopped snowing last night, this mouse left its nest and began hunting for food."

"Oh, I see," said Jane. "Its feet made the little round tracks. But what made the wavy mark between?"

"It dragged its tail," said Dad. "This mouse had a longer tail than some. It was probably a little white-footed mouse. Meadow mice don't have such long tails, so they make tracks just with their feet. Sometimes when the snow is deeper, mice make tunnels under the snow."

"Tracks are interesting," said Jane. "Let's look for some more."

"Oh, there are some big tracks!" cried Jane, as they were walking on. "Those are dog tracks. Topsy must have made them."

"Right," said Dad. "Topsy must have come out early. But look at these other tracks. Topsy was chasing a rabbit."

"Do you see the difference between these rabbit tracks and the mouse tracks?" he asked.

"Well, the rabbit tracks are larger," said Jane. "And the mouse tracks were all the same size."

"That's right," said Dad. "Notice how the rabbit's front feet make just one track or two tracks very close together. That is because a rabbit puts both front feet down close together. As it jumps, its big hind feet spread out and come down ahead of its front feet. Rabbit tracks seem to go backwards.

"Here are some other tracks," he said. "They do not show where the animal came from or where it went."

"I know those tracks," said Jane. "They are sparrow tracks. The sparrow flew down and hopped a little, and then flew away."

As she was eating breakfast Jane said, "I see what the poem meant by 'winter's picture book.' We could learn a lot about what the animals did last night. Do all animals come out at night to hunt for food?"

"Some animals store food in summer and autumn," said Dad. "They don't have to come out for food."

"Oh, we learned about them in school. Chipmunks store food, and squirrels do, too," said Jane.

"Good!" said Dad. "Mice and rabbits don't store food, so they have to come out and hunt for it in winter. On sunny days chipmunks and squirrels may come out."

"Chipmunks, rabbits, and squirrels are gnawing animals," said Jane.

"So are mice," said Dad.

"Some gnawing animals store food and some of them don't," said Jane.

"I know a gnawing animal whose tracks you'd never see in winter," said Dad. "It doesn't store food and it doesn't hunt for food."

"I know," cried Jane. "It's a woodchuck! A woodchuck hibernates."

"I'm going to ask Mr. Thorne if we can't go on a track hunt some day," said Jane.

If you found these tracks in the snow, could you tell which animals made them?

① ② ③ ④ ⑤ ⑥

Pictures in the Winter Sky

"Look, Hal," said Jack, "I found the notebook I made last year. Look at these star pictures. Aren't they funny? I'll bet I could draw them much better now."

"You ought to be able to draw better. You are a year older, you know," said Hal. "Do you remember the names of these groups of stars?"

"Let's see," said Jack. "This group makes a sky picture that looks like a dipper. It is called the Big Dipper. This one is called Cassiopeia. This picture is the Little Dipper."

"You are old enough now to know the right name for all sky pictures," said Cowboy Hal. "When a group of stars makes a pattern in the sky like these you have drawn, it is called a *constellation*."

"Whew! that's a big word," said Jack. "But I like it. Constellation—constellation. Let's go out and look for constellations."

"All right," laughed Cowboy Hal.

"Can you find the North Star, Jack?" he asked when they were out of doors.

"There it is," said Jack. "It is near the Big Dipper. It is a part of the Little Dipper. The Dippers are always in the north."

"That's right," said Cowboy Hal. "The Big Dipper always helps you find the North Star. If you should draw a line from the two stars in the front of the Dipper, the line would point to the North Star. Those two stars in the Dipper are called the *pointers*. They always point to the North Star."

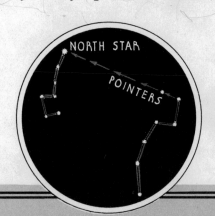

"That is an easy way to find the North Star," said Jack. "The Big Dipper is always easy to find. The pointers tell me which way to look for the North Star. Do they point toward the North Star in the spring when the Dipper is upside down?"

"The pointers still point to the North Star," said Cowboy Hal.

The next night Jack wanted to look at the stars again. He wanted to see if he could find the North Star. He thought it might help him find his way at night without a compass.

There were no clouds in the sky. It was a good night to look at the stars. Jack looked along the horizon for the Big Dipper.

"There it is, Hal," he cried, "and there is the North Star. I'm looking right at it."

"So you are," said Cowboy Hal. "If you hold
out your arms you can be a boy-compass."

Jack held out his arms. He was still looking at
the North Star.

"When I face the north, my right hand points
to the east," said Jack. "My left hand points to
the west. There is only one more direction. The
back of my head must be toward the south."

"That's fine," said Cowboy Hal, "but the needle
of a compass always points north and south. If
you face east, your arms will be pointing like a
compass needle."

"I can always find my way at night if I can see the stars," said Jack. "That is a good thing to know if I am ever lost or ever fly an airplane."

"Indeed it is," said Cowboy Hal. "There was a newspaper story during the war about a bomber crew finding its way back to its base. It was guided by the stars. Most army and navy planes have at least one crew member who can find his way by the stars."

"If I am going to fly an airplane when I am old enough, I must learn much more about the stars," said Jack. "Are there any more constellations, Hal?"

"Oh, yes," said Cowboy Hal. "There are many, many of them. The shepherds in olden times used to camp under the stars. They gave names to the brightest ones. Sometimes they told interesting stories about the constellations."

"I remember a story you told me about Orion," said Jack. "Can we see Orion tonight?"

"Orion is the most beautiful winter constellation," said Cowboy Hal. "The shepherds thought Orion looked like a man in the sky. Look toward the southeast and you will see him."

Jack made himself into a compass. He turned half way between east and south, and looked up at the sky. These are the stars that Jack saw first.

"It's hard for me to see a man, Hal," said Jack. "I see three bright stars in a row. There are three little stars below the big ones."

"You're getting pretty close," said Cowboy Hal. "The three larger stars are Orion's belt. The little stars are his sword hanging from his belt."

"Then those two bright stars up high are his arms," cried Jack.

"They are his shoulders," corrected Cowboy Hal.
"The bright star on the left that looks red is called
Betelgeuse. Betelgeuse is one of the largest stars
that we can see. It is very far away. Have you
found the stars that make Orion's knees?"

"Yes," said Jack. "They are very far apart."

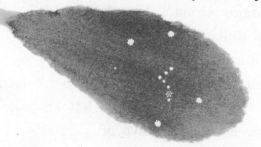

Jack could imagine that Orion, the hunter, looked
like this.

"Orion looks as though he is running after something," said Jack.

"He isn't running," said Cowboy Hal. "He is bracing himself for a charge."

Jack laughed. It was fun to imagine that Orion was going to fight.

"Who is charging Orion?" he asked.

"Taurus, the Bull," replied Cowboy Hal.

"Where is Taurus?" asked Jack.

"He's running at Orion's left shoulder," said Cowboy Hal. "Look above Orion's left shoulder. That bright star is the right eye of Taurus."

"Doesn't Taurus have a left eye?" asked Jack.

"Oh, yes," said Cowboy Hal, "but he's winking it. It isn't so bright as his right one."

These are the stars that Jack saw.

"All we can see is the Bull's head and his front legs," said Jack.

"That's right," said Cowboy Hal, "unless you think of those six little stars above his left eye as part of his back."

"Oh, I see them," said Jack. "Do they have a name, too?"

"Yes," answered Cowboy Hal. "They are called the Seven Sisters."

"Seven Sisters?" asked Jack. "You said there were six of them."

"There really are seven," said Cowboy Hal. "The men who study stars look at them through a powerful instrument called a *telescope*. With the telescope, the men can see seven stars. The seventh is too far away for most of us to see without a telescope."

"I remember that when we were studying birds we used field glasses to make the birds look larger," said Jack.

"That's right, you did," said Cowboy Hal. "If you look at the Seven Sisters with a telescope, the stars will look larger, too."

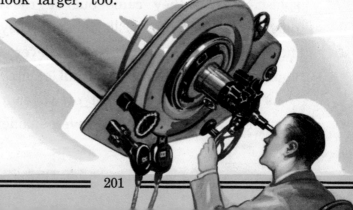

"Why are they called the Seven Sisters?" asked Jack.

"Long ago the Greek shepherds named these stars the Seven Daughters of Atlas. They imagined that the sisters were changed into doves to escape Orion, who was pursuing them. Indians tell a story about the Seven Sisters, too. This is their story."

The Seven Sisters

Long ago when there were few people on the earth, there was an Indian warrior named Elk. He lived with his uncle by the side of a wide river.

There was a broad sandy beach along the river. Many times young Elk slept on the beach under the stars. One night he thought he saw seven lights dancing on the river. He crept down close to the water. He saw seven maidens frolicking in the shallow water along the shore. They dipped into the water so silently that there wasn't even a splash. Then they came out on the beach and played on the sand. Elk thought they were the most beautiful maidens he had ever seen. The youngest was the most beautiful of all.

As Elk watched, a basket of woven reeds came down from the sky. The seven maidens seemed to float right into the basket and were drawn up to the sky. It all happened so quickly that when Elk turned his head, he saw them as seven twinkling stars in the sky.

The next night Elk watched the sisters again. The youngest maiden was so beautiful that Elk wanted her for his wife. Just as they were moving into the basket this time, Elk rushed out and tried to catch the youngest one. But he wasn't quick enough. The seven sisters were frightened. Each night they moved higher and higher in the sky. They did not come near the water.

Finally, when the blossoms were coming out on the first flowers, the Seven Sisters came near the western edge of the river. Elk watched them frolic on the beach again. They were even more beautiful than he had remembered. For a moment, he almost forgot that he wanted the youngest one for his wife. Just as the basket dipped down for them, he sprang like a flash and caught the beautiful little maiden.

"What do you want of me?" she asked.

"I have watched you and your sisters for many moons," said Elk, "and I have seen no Indian maiden so beautiful as you are. I want you to be my wife."

"I will be your wife," she said, "and live with you in your lodge. But first we must go to the house of the Sun, my father, and have our wedding feast." So Elk and the maiden were married.

After many moons on the earth, Elk and his wife went to live in the sky. To this day there are seven starry lights twinkling in the winter sky. Six of them shine clearly, but the seventh is too dim to see. She is Elk's wife, who lost her brightness by living on the earth. You can also see Elk, the mighty hunter, following the shining maidens.

"Orion was a hunter, too," said Jack, as Cowboy Hal finished the story.

"Yes," said Cowboy Hal, "Orion and Elk are names for the same constellation."

"I like that story as much as the one about Taurus, the Bull, don't you?" asked Jack.

"There are many more stories about the constellations," said Cowboy Hal. "They are all interesting."

"Why can't we see Orion in the summer?" asked Jack.

"Because the earth is moving around the sun," said Hal. "You know that the sun seems to move as the earth turns. If you could watch the stars all night, they would seem to move, too. In twenty-four hours the dippers would seem to swing around the North Star. Orion seems to rise in the east and set in the west. We know that Orion does not move in relation to the earth, any more than the sun moves. It only seems to move because the earth is turning. But the earth also moves around the sun. We see constellations at different times of the year, depending on where the earth is in relation to the sun. An experiment will help you to understand. Let's go into the house to do it.

"Pretend that your head is the earth and the light on the table is the sun. Let that picture on the wall be a constellation. Where will you stand so you can see the constellation best?"

"Here," said Jack, as he stood between the lamp and the picture. "The sun is back of me. It is night. I am facing the constellation."

"Yes," said Cowboy Hal. "That is the way you see Orion in winter. Now start moving around the sun."

Jack moved left around the table.

"Stop," said Hal. "Where is the constellation now?"

Jack looked at the picture.

"The constellation is on my right. It is in the west," he said.

"That is where you see Orion in the spring," said Hal.

Jack moved on around the table. When he was opposite his starting place, he stopped. "The

constellation is on the other side of the sun," he said. "I can't see it at night."

"Yes," said Cowboy Hal. "Now it is summer. The constellation is still in the sky, but you can't see it. Let's go out and look at the sky again."

Outside, Jack was very quiet. It all seemed so wonderful. He had to think and try to understand.

He was looking at the Seven Sisters. "The stars in the Seven Sisters are very small," he said. "They must be very far away."

"They are," said Hal, "but not so far away as many other stars. Look at the Milky Way."

Jack looked at the big white band that stretched across the sky from northeast to southwest.

"It looks like a thin cloud, doesn't it?" he said.

"It does look something like a cloud," said Cowboy Hal, "but it isn't. It is made of more stars than anybody can count. They are so far away that we can't see them plainly."

Jack's neck hurt because he had been looking up so long. He was glad to look back at Orion again. Suddenly he pointed to a very bright star below Orion's feet.

"Oh, Hal," he cried, "there is the brightest star we have seen. It must be a big one."

"It is big," said Cowboy Hal, "but not so big as Betelgeuse. It looks large because it is the nearest of all the stars we can see from our part of the earth. The shepherds thought it was Orion's dog. They called it the Dog Star. Its name is Sirius."

"It seems to change color." said Jack. "How bright it is!"

Jack's head was full of new ideas. Before he went to bed, he drew new pictures in his notebook of all the constellations Cowboy Hal had showed him. Jack's notebook looked like this. How many of these constellations can you name?

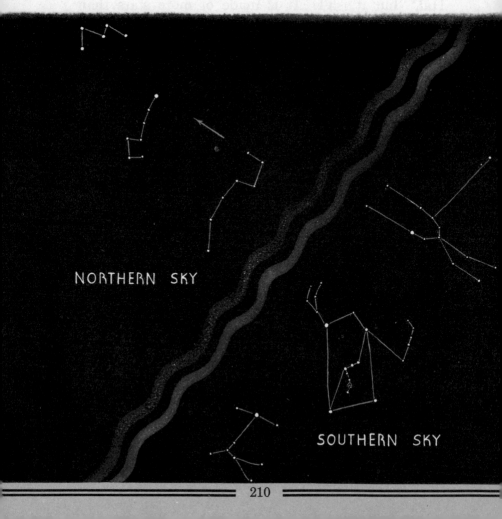

NORTHERN SKY

SOUTHERN SKY

The Sun, the Moon, and the Earth

The children were seeing who could throw a ball highest into the air. Dick could throw it higher than anybody else. He could throw a ball over the schoolhouse.

"I wish I could throw it so high we couldn't see it," said Dick, as he tried again. "I wish I could throw it so high it wouldn't come down."

"Nobody could do that," said Jimmy. "No matter how high you could throw it, it would still come down to the ground."

"Yes," laughed Susan. "My father says that everything that goes up must come down."

Just then it was time to go back to school. The children were still talking about the ball when they reached their room.

"Mr. Thorne," asked Dick, "is it true that everything that goes up must come down?"

"Can you think of anything that doesn't fall to the ground?" asked Mr. Thorne.

The children tried to think of something that wouldn't fall. They couldn't think of a thing.

"I know why things fall to the ground," said Jimmy. "The earth pulls them."

"That is right," said Mr. Thorne. "The earth pulls everything toward itself. The earth's pull is called *gravity*. It is the earth's gravity that holds you on the ground. It is the earth's gravity that pulls your ball down when you throw it."

"The earth pulls us something like a magnet, doesn't it, Mr. Thorne?" asked Jane.

"That is a good comparison," said Mr. Thorne. "But why do you say *something* like a magnet, Jane?"

"It isn't exactly like a magnet. Magnets pull only certain metals. The earth pulls many different things," said Jane.

"Yes, the earth pulls everything," said Mr. Thorne.

Gravity holds you to the earth. If there were no gravity, you would not stay on the earth."

"Then it's gravity that brings me back to the ground when I do my high-jump," said Bob.

Everybody laughed then.

Bob laughed, too.

"The earth's gravity is even strong enough to pull one of the nearest heavenly bodies," continued Mr. Thorne.

"The nearest heavenly body is the moon," said Jimmy.

"That's right," said Mr. Thorne. "The moon is always moving around the earth. If it weren't for gravity, the moon would fly off into space, too."

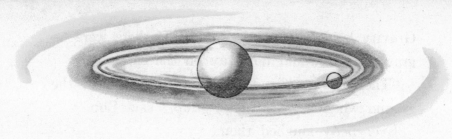

"Could we do an experiment to prove that?" asked Bob.

"I think so," said Mr. Thorne. "Let's imagine that this eraser is the moon. You can be the earth, Bob. Tie the eraser to one end of a string. You hold the other end, Bob. Now turn around just as fast as you can."

This is how Bob looked.

"You see," said Mr. Thorne, "the eraser can't get away from Bob as long as he holds the string."

"I see," said Jane. "Then the moon can't get away from the earth as long as there is gravity."

"How long does it take the moon to travel around the earth?" asked Nancy.

"About a month," said Dick.

"The Indians used to measure time by the moon," said Mr. Thorne. "As the moon moves around the earth we see it part of the time. Only one side of it is lighted."

"It's the sun that lights the moon," said Jane. "The moon has no light of its own."

"Yes, that is right," said Mr. Thorne. "The moon is cold and dark. Come over here and look at that white building across the street. The sunlight shines on this corner of it. The white wall makes the light shine back in our eyes. When the sun shines on it, the white wall seems to have light of its own."

"The moon is like the white wall," said Mr. Thorne. "It catches the sunlight and makes it shine back on the earth. We say it *reflects* the sunlight. We call the light moonlight, but it is really *reflected* sunlight."

Everybody went back to his seat but Jimmy. He made a fist with his right hand and put out his arm at full length. Then he began to turn around and around. Then he said, "May we make the room dark, Mr. Thorne, and turn on the desk light?"

Then he turned around again.

"I think I've learned something else, Mr. Thorne," he said. "I'm imagining that the desk light is the sun. My head is the earth. My fist is the moon. When the moon goes around the earth, it gets between the sun and the earth. It makes a shadow on the earth."

"We have a particular name for a shadow like that," said Mr. Thorne. "We call it an eclipse of the sun. When there is a total eclipse of the sun, it is like night on the earth. The air gets cooler. We can see the stars. Even the chickens and birds go to roost. When there is a total eclipse, the sun looks like this."

Mr. Thorne showed the children a picture.

"Most savages were afraid of an eclipse. They thought something terrible was going to happen. They were afraid that a great dragon was going to eat the sun. They beat on their drums and shouted to scare the dragon away. When the eclipse was over, they were happy. They thought they had saved the sun. We aren't afraid now. We know the moon is just making a shadow on the earth."

When Mr. Thorne finished the story, all the children did Jimmy's experiment to show what an eclipse of the sun is like.

"I think I understand now how the earth and the moon go around the sun together," said Bob. "I'll draw a picture of them."

MOON

EARTH

SUN

The Eclipse of the Moon

"Did you see the eclipse of the moon last night, Mr. Thorne?" asked Jimmy.

"Yes, I did," said Mr. Thorne. "I watched it all the time it lasted."

Jimmy had never before seen an eclipse. He wanted to know more about it.

"Did anyone else see the eclipse?" asked Mr. Thorne.

"I did," said Bob and Susan at the same time. The other children had not seen the eclipse.

"We learned what makes an eclipse of the sun," said Susan. "What makes an eclipse of the moon?"

"We can find out," said Mr. Thorne. "First, what do you know about the moon?"

"It is a heavenly body," said Bob.

"It travels around the earth," said Nancy.

"It has no light of its own," said Jimmy.

"Then where does moonlight come from?" asked Susan.

"Light from the sun falls on the moon," said Jimmy. "Then the light comes to us from the moon."

"Moonlight is reflected sunlight," said Jane.

"Oh, now I remember about that," said Susan. "We can see the moon only when the sun shines on it. But what happens in an eclipse?"

"The moon moves into a shadow," said Bob. "Here, I will show you what I saw last night. I read in the paper that the eclipse would begin at ten o'clock. At ten o'clock the moon looked like this.

"It was big and full. Then it began to move into a shadow. It looked like this.

"It kept moving farther and farther into the shadow until it was almost covered.

"Then it moved out of the shadow.

"After a while the moon looked just the way it had looked at ten o'clock.

"The eclipse was over. It had lasted nearly an hour."

"I want to know two things," said Jimmy. "First, what made the shadow; and second, how did anybody know the eclipse would happen at exactly ten o'clock last night?"

"The shadow was made by the earth. The eclipse was caused by the moon's getting in the earth's shadow," said Mr. Thorne.

"You remember that the moon travels around the earth. At times the moon is on the side of the earth away from the sun and the sun's rays can not reach it. The moon is in the earth's shadow. Here, I will show you on the blackboard."

SUN

EARTH   MOON

"Then an eclipse of the moon is really the shadow of the earth on the moon," said Jimmy.

"Yes, that is right," said Mr. Thorne. "And the shadow is round because the earth is round. When you are in a movie, someone ahead of you may get up. You can see his shadow on the movie screen.

The shadow is shaped like the man's head. The shadow on the moon is round because the earth is round."

"How did anybody know that the eclipse was to come at ten o'clock?" asked Jimmy.

"That was easy," said Dick. "It was printed right on the calendar. See, our school calendar shows when the eclipse was to come."

The children looked at the calendar.

"Then someone must have known about this eclipse a long time ago," said Jimmy.

"That is right," said Mr. Thorne. "It is possible to tell the exact minute an eclipse is to come. It is possible to know many years ahead of its happening."

"How can we know so far ahead?" asked Nancy.

"By studying the sun, the earth, and the moon," said Mr. Thorne. "Scientists have found out through long years of study the exact movements of the heavenly bodies. They can tell years ahead just when the sun will rise on any certain day. They can tell what the movements of the moon and the earth are to be. They know just how the stars will move and where and when they will appear."

Weather Changes Rocks and Soil

The high-school boys and girls who were studying aviation had a little airplane to experiment with. It was kept on a field just behind the schoolhouse. During the winter months the plane had been in the hangar and the field was deserted. Now the winter was over. The snow was all gone. The weather was warm. It was time to fly! But the field that had been so carefully kept clean the last summer was now covered with stones. There were stones even on the runways.

"I thought we helped the high-school students clear all the stones off that field last spring," said Jimmy. "Now look at it, will you?"

The boys decided to ask Mr. Thorne about it. When the How and Why Club met that morning, Bob said, "Mr. Thorne, we have a problem we can't solve."

"What is it?" asked their science teacher. "Perhaps we can solve it together."

"It's the flying field," said Bob. "It's all covered with stones. Last spring we cleared every stone off the whole field. Now it is covered again. May we go out there this morning?"

So the How and Why Club had its meeting on the flying field. When they were all there, Mr. Thorne said, "Now, Bob, you may tell us what your problem is."

"Last spring we helped the high-school students clear this land and make this flying field. We picked up every stone. There was not one there all summer. This morning Jimmy and I discovered that the field is again covered with stones."

"It seems as though the rocks come to the surface during the winter," said Nancy.

"That's just what they do!" exclaimed Jimmy. "Why didn't we think of that before! Things freeze in winter. Freezing makes water expand. I have often seen milk that has frozen in the bottle. The freezing makes the milk expand. The stopper is pushed right out of the bottle."

"I have another example of what freezing does," said Susan. "A new concrete sidewalk was laid in front of our house last summer. Last winter one of the big blocks was pushed up in the center and cracked. There was water in the ground under the sidewalk. When it froze, it expanded and the concrete block was broken."

"That has been happening here," said Bob. "The water in the ground froze during the winter. As it expanded, these rocks were pushed out of the ground. The force of expanding water pushed them."

"That is part of the process," said Mr. Thorne. "Cold weather affected this field in other ways. As the rocks were forced through the soil, little pieces of dirt stuck to them. When the snow melted, the water ran over the rocks. The water washed the dirt back to the ground. It washed tiny pieces of rock off, too. These became part of the soil."

"Is that why all these stones are rounded and smooth?" asked Nancy.

"No," said Mr. Thorne. "Rolling over and over in a stream could make them smooth. As they rolled, the sand in the stream would rub against them. Most of these stones have been rounded by moving ice."

"Please tell us more about how it happened," said Susan.

"It happened many, many years ago," said Mr. Thorne. "Try to imagine a snowstorm that lasted for weeks and weeks. Instead of covering one town or state, it covered the whole northern part of America. The snow fell until it was as deep as Mr. Ross's barn. Still it kept on falling until it was many times deeper. The pressure on the snow near the ground was so great that ice formed."

"That's what happens when we squeeze snowballs too hard," said Dick. "They are almost like balls of ice."

"Finally," continued Mr. Thorne, "the ice became very thick. Perhaps it was many hundreds of feet thick. Such a mass of ice is called a *glacier*. A

glacier moves slowly. As it moves along, it pushes dirt and stones ahead of it. It crushes other stones to powdery soil by its great weight. It is thought that the smooth stones you see here were rounded by a great glacier or ice sheet."

"Did the ice sheet cover all of North America?" asked Nancy.

"No," answered Mr. Thorne. "It covered Canada and the northern part of the United States.

"Some people think a great change came in the climate of the country. The air grew warmer. The ice began to melt. Where it melted there were huge piles of rock and soil that had been carried hundreds of miles. Some of these stones you see here may have rolled over and over under the ice until they rubbed off their sharp edges."

"Back of the school there are lots of stones. Some of them are round. Some of them have flat sides, with big scratches in them," said Nancy. "Were they carried here, too?"

"We think so," said Mr. Thorne. "They were probably carried along for hundreds of miles."

"Cold weather and snow and ice have helped a lot in making our soil," said Jimmy. "Last year we learned that water freezing in cracks of rocks sometimes breaks the rocks apart. When rocks are broken into small pieces they help make soil."

"And snow does something else for the soil that we haven't mentioned yet," said Bob. "When snow melts, the water soaks into the ground. It makes the ground moist for growing plants. In places where the sun doesn't shine, like a woods or the shady side of a house, the snow doesn't melt very fast. It keeps adding moisture to the ground long after a snowstorm."

"That may be true for shady places," said Dick, "but I found a hillside where the snow melted very rapidly in the sun. We can see it on our way back to school. Would you like to stop and look at it?"

The children were interested in the hill Dick showed them.

"This is a good example of what running water does to soil," said Mr. Thorne. "Notice that near the top of the hill very little dirt has been washed away. The melted snow made only a tiny stream up there. As it ran down the hillside the stream became much larger and went faster and faster. At the bottom of the hill it made this big gully."

"And here is the dirt that was washed out of the hill," called Jimmy. "It is all piled up here on the level. Even the big stones were washed down. The fine dirt and sand have been washed out farther than the stones."

"There is a reason for that," said Mr. Thorne. "Moving water carries soil. Slow-moving water carries some soil. Fast-moving water carries more.

"The water running down this hill was moving very fast. It had enough force to carry stones as well as soil. As soon as the water reached the level ground, it slowed down. It was not running fast enough to carry the stones. They were dropped at the foot of the hill. The fine sand and soil were not so heavy. The water carried them farther and dropped them."

"I remember seeing a hill that Father plowed last spring," said Dick. "He had just leveled it off when a heavy rain came. All down the side of the hill were little streams where the water washed away the loose dirt."

"When water washes dirt away like that we call it *erosion*," said Mr. Thorne. "All flowing water causes some kind of erosion. Rivers constantly wash away soil."

"This must have looked like a small river when the snow was melting," said Jimmy, pointing to the gully.

"Rivers start in places like this," said Mr. Thorne. "Usually they start in the mountains where there is

snow all year, or where there are springs. The water runs down the mountain side. The river becomes larger as it flows along. Sometimes it breaks off pieces of stone and rolls them along. As the rushing water scrapes and rolls the stones along the river bottom, the solid rock underneath is gradually worn away. The broken rocks are worn smooth and round. The river cuts its way through the rocks and soil just as this water has cut away the bank."

Back at school once more, Mr. Thorne showed the children some pictures of a river that started in the mountains. "This is a mountain river that has cut its way through solid rock," he said. "This river has been wearing away the rock for thousands of years. It has finally made this deep gorge."

"What happened to all the rock and fine particles that have been worn away?" asked Bob.

"The force of the rushing water carried much of it downstream," said Mr. Thorne. "When the river reached the less mountainous ground, it ran more slowly. It dropped its fine particles of rocks and soil. This soil finally filled in the lowland along the course of the river and made this broad level valley."

"Is erosion still going on?" asked Jane.

"I can answer that," said Jimmy. "As long as water is moving, the erosion goes on. The water wears away rock in the mountains. It also wears away the dirt from its banks. When it flows fast, it wears away so much dirt that the water becomes muddy. Erosion goes on all the time."

The Workshop

The children were much excited one January day. The new school workshop was to be opened for the first time. Jimmy, Bob, and Dick were all planning to build model airplanes. The girls were just as busy discussing the things they were going to make.

"I have helped Dad at home," said Bob, "but he never lets me use his tools unless he is right there to watch me. Now I will have my own."

"Your father is wise," said Mr. Thorne. "Unless you know how to use tools properly, you shouldn't try to use them. Do you know why?"

"We might get hurt," said Jimmy.

"That is right," said Mr. Thorne. "It is time for you to go to shop now. I shall go with you and introduce your shop teacher."

The children went with Mr. Thorne. "Mr. Jackson, here is a new group for you," Mr. Thorne said, as he opened the door to the shop. "They're a fine group of boys and girls. They are anxious to work in the shop."

Mr. Jackson smiled. "I am glad to have them," he replied. "Come in, boys and girls, and we'll get acquainted."

When the children went into the shop they saw many interesting things. They saw workbenches with different kinds of tools on them. They saw machines to help in making all kinds of things. They saw a lathe, a vise, and a paper-cutting machine. "You may walk around a few minutes and look," said Mr. Jackson, "but don't touch anything until I have a chance to show you how. When you

have finished looking, come back to this table. We'll talk about the tools."

When the children gathered around the table again, Mr. Jackson said, "Since this is the first time you have been in a shop, we need to discuss some of the things in this room."

"This is your workroom. Everything in it has been put here for the boys and girls of this school to use. Many boys and girls will use these materials every day. What is the first thing to remember?"

"To take care of the tools," said Bob.

"Yes," said Mr. Jackson. "That is important. We should take care of the tools and the machines. But there is something else."

"We must not waste paper or wood," said Nancy.

"That is right. We must use all of our materials carefully. If we all cooperate, the school will be able to supply what we need to use but there will not be enough to waste. Then there is another important thing we must learn. Many of the tools and machines we are using are new to you."

"We have to know how to use them," said Susan, "or we might break them."

"Not only because you might break them," said Mr. Jackson, "but because you might hurt yourselves. Here are some tools that you are going to use.

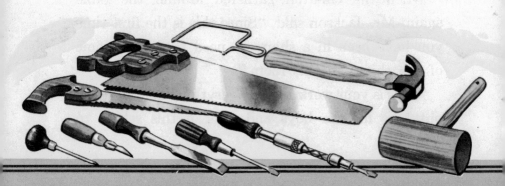

What are some of the ways they might hurt you?"

"Some of them are sharp," said Bob. "If you are using a knife, you should always whittle away from you. If you whittle toward you, the knife might slip. Then you'd cut yourself."

"When you are sawing you should keep your left hand away from the saw," said Jimmy.

"You should also hold the board firmly," said Mr. Jackson, "so it won't slip.

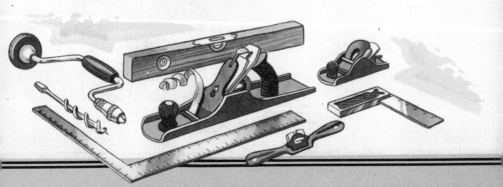

"As we work with each new tool, I'll show you how to use it," said Mr. Jackson, "but always remember these things about sharp tools. Never pull them toward you. Keep your fingers away from their sharp edges. Be sure the handles are not loose. Hold the tool firmly. Hold the materials you are working with securely. Now, what are some other ways that tools may hurt you?"

"You could pound your fingers," said Susan.

The boys laughed. "Girls can't drive nails," said Jimmy.

"Oh, yes, they can," said Mr. Jackson. "They can learn to put the nail in straight, then to hit the nail squarely and to keep their fingers out of the

way. You also need to be careful of boards that have nails in them. Never leave them lying with the nails up. Someone might step or fall on them.

"You need to learn to keep out of each other's way. Each of you must watch to see that someone else isn't going to be hurt by a tool he is using.

"In case there is an accident, report it to me at once. I have a first aid kit and can fix up cuts and bruises. The best first aid is to prevent accidents."

"Let's have an honor roll for people who prevent accidents," said Bob.

"That's a good suggestion, Bob," said Mr. Jackson. "How would we do it?"

"Well," said Bob, "we can have a list of our names on a chart. Each day we take care of our tools and use them properly we can put a credit mark after our names. At the end of the month everyone with credit marks for every day can be on the honor roll."

"We might call it a Safety Club," suggested Susan. "Then other classes could belong, too."

"Those are excellent suggestions," said Mr. Jackson. "Perhaps Mr. Thorne will let you make a chart. You can bring it with you tomorrow. Tomorrow we will start using our tools."

Rainbow Colors

In summer there is seldom any rain where Rita and Pablo live. All of the river beds are dry. They become white ribbons of sand that sparkle and shine in the hot bright sun. They look like the picture.

One afternoon Rita and Pablo decided to explore the banks of the dry river near their home. They met Mr. Harris, a man from the United States experimental farm. It was fun to walk along with Mr. Harris. It was fun to kick through the white sand. The sand was hot on the children's feet. It was bright in their eyes.

"Pablo, I think we had better go home," said Rita after a while. "I have a headache. The sun is too bright. It hurts my eyes."

"Put on my big hat," said Pablo. "That will keep the sun out of your eyes."

Rita put on Pablo's big hat. "That helps a little," she said, "but my eyes still hurt when I look at the sand. This white sand is almost as bright as the sun."

"The sand is so bright where the sun shines on it," said Pablo, "that it is almost like having the sun shine in your face."

"And it is so white," said Rita. "I wonder what makes it look so white."

"Let's see if you can figure it out," said Mr. Harris. "We couldn't see the sand if it weren't for the light. Where does the light come from?"

"From the sun, of course," said Rita.

"The sun's rays help us to see most things," said Mr. Harris. "There are some things we can't see, though, even with the sun's rays shining on them. Sometimes when the sun shines on clear glass, the rays go right through the glass. When light rays shine through an object, we can't see the object."

"Guess what happened to me the other day," said Pablo. "I stopped to look in a store window. I almost bumped my head on the glass. The glass was so clear I didn't see it."

"Exactly," said Mr. Harris. "The light rays went right through the glass so you didn't know the glass was there."

"The sun's rays do not shine through all objects," continued Mr. Harris. "When the sun's rays shine on some things, the light from them shines back into our eyes. We see such things only when the light comes back from them to our eyes. Light that shines back into our eyes from any object is reflected light."

"Then that's why the sand in the river bed seems so bright. The sun's rays shine on the sand and are reflected into our eyes," said Rita.

"Yes," said Mr. Harris. "The sand reflects so much of the light from the sun that it looks white."

"That must be why a concrete road looks so white," said Pablo. "When we rode into town the other day I noticed that the white concrete road made the light shine back into my eyes. My eyes didn't hurt when we drove on the black road. Why was that?"

"The black road reflects very little light," said Mr. Harris. "A road that reflects all the light that shines on it looks white. A road that reflects only a little light may look dark or even black."

"Can we perform an experiment to show how light is reflected?" asked Pablo.

"That will be easy," said Mr. Harris. "We will perform an experiment when we get to your house."

When they were inside, Mr. Harris said, "The sun is shining through the front window. Pull down the curtain, Pablo."

There was a tiny hole in the curtain. Only a narrow ray of light shone through to the table.

"Now see what happens when you put a piece of smooth white paper where the light can shine on it," said Mr. Harris.

"The light shines on the paper and then shines on the wall," said Pablo. "It is reflected from the white paper to the wall."

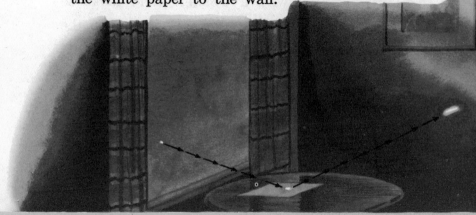

When Pablo put a piece of black paper under the light, there was no reflection. "That proves what we said about the white road and the black road," he said. "Black paper doesn't reflect much light. The black road doesn't reflect much light."

"What happens when light shines on water?" asked Rita.

"Water has many effects on light," said Mr. Harris. "In the first place, water reflects some of the light. You have seen how bright the river looks when the sun shines on it. But I will show you what happens when a ray of sunlight strikes drops of water. Let's go out of doors."

Mr. Harris turned on the sprinkler. This is what the children saw as soon as the sun struck the fountain of water.

"It's a rainbow," cried the children.

"Yes, it is a rainbow," said Mr. Harris. "Rays of light are not only reflected when they strike tiny drops of water. They may be broken up into colors. Then we see violet, indigo, blue, green, yellow, orange, and red.

"Rainbows appear in the sky only when the sunlight strikes tiny drops of water," Mr. Harris went on. "The rays of the sunlight are broken up into the rainbow colors. All the colors are in the ray but when we see them together, they look white."

"Thank you, Mr. Harris, for telling us about it," said Pablo. "I'm going to ask Miss Bennett if she will tell our class about it tomorrow."

The next day as soon as class had started, Pablo said, "Miss Bennett, yesterday Mr. Harris showed us some interesting things about light. He told us that we see objects by reflected light. Sunlight looks white to us, but it really has seven different colors in it. He made a rainbow with the lawn sprinkler to show us the colors. I think the rest of the class would like to know about sunlight, too."

"Can you show the class some of the things you learned?" asked Miss Bennett.

Pablo pulled down the shade until just a ray of light came in. He performed his experiments with white and black paper to show how rays of light are reflected.

"Can you see where the light comes in?" asked Miss Bennett.

"Through the crack under the shade," said Pablo.

"You can't see it," said Rita.

"I think you could catch some of it in your hand," said Miss Bennett.

The children laughed. Pablo moved his hand back and forth in the ray. When it was in the ray the children could see the light.

"Light has to be reflected before you can see it," said Pablo.

Miss Bennett made some chalk dust in the air.

"The chalk dust reflects the light," said Rita.

"If we can go outside, we can see colors in the spray from the lawn sprinkler," said Pablo.

"We don't have to go outside to make the colors of the rainbow," said Miss Bennett. "Here is a piece of glass called a *prism*. Hold it in the sunlight."

Pablo held the prism where the rays of the sun could pass through it. The children saw colors of the rainbow where the light fell on the table. The prism had separated the colors of the white light.

"Those are the same colors that we saw in the rainbow yesterday," said Rita. "I don't understand why we don't see them all the time, though."

"When all these colors are in one ray, the ray looks white," explained Miss Bennett. "Here is a card that has all the colors on it. Hold it so that everyone can see it, Rita, and then spin it around fast."

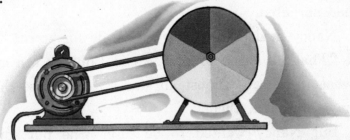

When Rita spun the card around the children couldn't see the different colors. The card looked white.

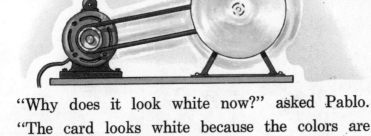

"Why does it look white now?" asked Pablo.

"The card looks white because the colors are mixed," said Miss Bennett. "They are mixed in your eyes when you look at them. When the card is still you look at each color, one color at a time. When it is whirled you see all the colors at once. Then they are mixed and look white."

Three Kinds of Sugar

The How and Why Club did an experiment. They put some corn and wheat seeds between pieces of wet blotting paper. They left the seeds until they had sprouted.

Nancy said, "Let's test the seeds for starch."

"That's a waste of time," said Bob. "Corn and wheat seeds are almost all starch. Of course they have starch in them."

But Nancy wanted to be sure. She put some iodine on the sprouting wheat seeds. "Oh," she cried, "there isn't much starch in them."

The children gathered around her. She dropped some iodine on the sprouting corn. There was not much starch in the sprouting corn, either.

"Where has the starch gone?" asked Jimmy.

"The little plants needed food to grow," said Mr. Thorne. "In a way, seeds are like your bodies. The starch you eat must be changed to sugar before you can use it. Do you remember the crackers you chewed? The starch partly changed to sugar in your mouth. The starch in corn and in wheat seeds must be changed to sugar before the little plants can use it."

"Has the starch changed to sugar?" asked Dick. "Is that why there's not much starch?"

"Why don't you chew some of the sprouting wheat and learn for yourself?" suggested Mr. Thorne.

Dick chewed a wheat seed. Jane chewed a corn seed.

"The wheat seed tastes sweet!" exclaimed Dick. "It must have sugar in it."

"The corn seed tastes sweet, too," said Jane. "The starch must have changed to sugar."

"Exactly," said Mr. Thorne. "The starch in these seeds had changed to sugar before you chewed them."

"Has the starch in the twigs changed to sugar by now?" asked Jimmy. "I believe I will go out and get a twig to test. I want to find out."

Jimmy split a maple twig and tested it for starch. "Look!" he cried, "last fall the iodine made a blue spot under each bud. A thin layer under the bark turned blue, too. Now the twig doesn't turn blue at all. The starch in the twig must have changed to sugar."

"Is that where maple sugar comes from?" asked Nancy.

"We get maple sugar from the kind of tree called the sugar maple," said Mr. Thorne. "We get the sugar from the sap of the tree. Sap is the juice that flows through a tree. The sap of a sugar-maple tree looks like water and it is sweet."

"I think I saw some sap today," said Nancy. "It looked like water dripping from a broken branch. Maybe the tree was a sugar maple."

"My grandfather has some sugar-maple trees," said Dick. "He taps them every spring to get the sap. Sap runs out of the holes. He catches the sap in buckets."

"What does he do with it?" asked Susan.

"He boils it and makes it into maple syrup," said Dick. "My grandfather sells a lot of maple syrup."

"Does he make maple sugar, too?" asked Susan.

"Yes, he makes some of the syrup into sugar," said Dick. "He sells maple sugar, too."

"I wish we could tap a sugar maple," said Susan. "It would be fun to make some maple sugar."

"You may," said Mr. Thorne. "There is a sugar maple right in front of the school building."

"Oh! that's where I saw the sap dripping," said Nancy.

The How and Why Club decided to do an experiment with maple sap. They decided to bring from home the things that they would need for the experiment.

They began their experiment the next day. Jimmy bored a hole through the bark of the tree. Dick put a spout into the hole. His grandfather had loaned him the spout.

Bob hung a bucket on the tree.

"How soon will the bucket be filled?" he asked.

"We will have to watch and see," said Jimmy. "Bob, you look into the bucket every hour during the day."

"I'd like to know where the sap is in the tree," said Nancy.

"It is in the wood just underneath the bark," said Dick. "That wood is called *sapwood*. The sap

SAPWOOD

rises in the sapwood in the spring. It flows into the hole. Then it flows through the spout and into the bucket."

"Won't the hole hurt the tree?" asked Jane.

"No," answered Mr. Thorne. "One hole in a tree will not harm it. But if we should put holes all around a tree, we would kill it. Water could not rise higher than the holes. The tree could not live without water."

When Bob came to school the next morning, he found the bucket full of sap. He carried the full bucket into the schoolroom and got another bucket to put under the spout.

Each of the children tasted the sap.

"My, it's good," said Nancy. "Let's make it into sugar."

When they had a big kettleful they boiled the sap. It boiled all day. The water in the sap evaporated as it boiled. The sap got thicker and thicker.

"Now it's syrup," said Jane. "Let's taste it."

Each child tasted the syrup. There was just a little syrup.

"My, it took a lot of sap," said Susan.

At last only the sugar crystals were left.

"I like maple sugar," said Jane, "but I never knew where it came from."

"Where does our other sugar come from?" asked Susan. "Does it come from trees, too?"

"Some sugar comes from sugar cane," said Jimmy, "but sugar cane doesn't grow around here."

"I've heard that some sugar comes from sugar beets," said Bob. "Sugar beets don't grow around here, either."

"I think we should write to someone who knows about sugar cane and sugar beets," said Jane. "Mr. Thorne, could you tell us where to send our letters?"

"Yes, indeed," said Mr. Thorne. "I know two children who live where sugar cane is grown. Their names are Martha Lou and Randy. And you know Rita and Pablo. Sugar beets are grown where they live. You write your letters. Then I will tell you where to send them."

These are the letters the children wrote:

Dear Martha Lou and Randy,

We are experimenting with plants that have sugar in them. Mr. Thorne, our teacher, says that you can tell us about sugar cane. We would like to know how sugar is made from sugar cane. We hope you can tell us.

Sincerely yours,
The How and Why Club

Dear Rita and Pablo,

You live in an interesting part of the country. Two years ago you sent us a horned toad. Now Mr. Thorne, our teacher, says you can tell us about sugar beets. We are experimenting with plants that have sugar stored in them. Please write to us and tell us how sugar is made from sugar beets.

Sincerely yours,
The How and Why Club

There was great excitement a few days later when the first answer arrived.

"This letter is from Martha Lou and Randy," said Jimmy as he opened it. "Nancy, you are the secretary of the club. Will you read the letter?"

The Letter from the South

Dear Children of the How and Why Club,

We received your letter. We are glad to tell you about sugar cane. We raise sugar cane on our farm. Sugar cane is a plant that stores sugar in its stem.

Sugar cane grows here because of the warm, damp climate. This is the way it is planted.

A piece of stem is put into the ground. The pieces are planted close together. A new plant grows from each piece.

Sugar cane grows very tall. It looks something like corn. But it grows much taller than corn.

It takes more than a year for sugar cane to grow. As it grows, it stores food in its stem. The food is sugar.

When the sugar cane is grown, it is cut down. The long stems are taken to a sugar mill. The stems are run through rollers. They look like the rollers that your mother runs her clothes through on wash day. The rollers press out most of the juice. The juice is boiled and boiled. The water in the juice evaporates and leaves crystals. The crystals are sugar crystals.

We like to chew on the stems of the sugar cane. The juice tastes sweet. We play that it is candy.

Your new friends,

Martha Lou and Randy

The Letter from the Southwest

Dear Children of the How and Why Club,

We were glad you wrote to us. Rita and I live on a sugar-beet farm. Our father raises sugar beets. I will tell you how he raises them.

Sugar beets grow from seeds. Father usually plants the seeds in April. He plants them very close together in straight rows. In May he blocks and thins the sugar beets. Perhaps you do not know what I mean by that. He uses a hoe that is eight inches wide. He hoes out eight inches of the little sugar-beet plants. Then he skips a little patch of plants and hoes out another eight inches. That is called *blocking*.

The hired man follows behind him. He thins the
beets. This is the way he does it. He pulls out
all but one beet in each patch that is left.

This is called *thinning*. He tries to pull out all
but the best plant. Then the best beet plant has
plenty of space to grow. Do you know that a sugar
beet stores food in its roots? It does, and that is why
it must have plenty of space to grow.

After they block and thin the beets, they keep the weeds from growing. Weeds take water that the beets need.

The beets grow all summer but they never get very tall. The leaves get large. The most important part of the beet is the root, for it has sugar in it. It is almost white. A full-grown beet weighs about two pounds.

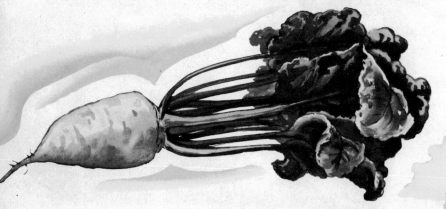

In the early fall Father pulls up the sugar beets. He cuts the tops off them. He throws the beets into piles. Then he puts them on his truck and takes them to the sugar factory. The factory is not far from our farm.

The sugar beets are cut up and cooked in the sugar factory. The sugar that was stored in the beets during the summer is cooked out and made into a juice. The juice is boiled and boiled until it is very thick. At last only sugar crystals are left. The sugar is put into sacks and sent to many parts of the United States.

Rita and I hope this will help you to understand how sugar is made from beets.

Sincerely yours,

Pablo

"Those are certainly interesting letters!" exclaimed Bob.

"Now we know about three different kinds of sugar," said Jimmy. "One kind comes from a tree. One comes from the root of a plant. And the other comes from the stem of a plant."

"And they are all made from the food that a plant has stored," said Jane.

"Let's send some of our maple sugar to these children," suggested Susan. "They probably don't have sugar maples in the places where they live."

The Club decided to do this. The girls packed some maple sugar in two boxes. The boys wrote the letters.

Dear Children,

We liked your letter about sugar. We have learned that sugar comes from sugar cane and sugar beets. We have a plant in Pleasant Valley that stores sugar, too. It is the sugar-maple tree.

The sugar maple stores starch in late summer. In spring, water mixes with the starch. The starch changes to sugar. Then it is called sap. The sap rises in the tree. It rises just under the bark. The sap goes to all parts of the tree. The tree uses the sap for food. The food helps the tree to grow.

We tapped a sugar-maple tree and collected some of the sap. It was sweet. We boiled it until it made sugar crystals. These sugar crystals are called maple sugar. We are sending some maple sugar to you. We hope you like it.

Sincerely yours,

The How and Why Club

Roots That Store Food

"We have learned about many plants that store starch," said Jimmy, at the next meeting of the How and Why Club. "The starch is changed to sugar before it is used by the plant. Are there any other plants that we might study?"

Mr. Thorne thought for a minute.

"Yes," he said, "there are several very common plants that are interesting ones to study. Many weeds, for instance, store food in their roots. They use the stored food during the winter. In the spring these weeds bloom very early. They are able to bloom before other flowers because they can use the food that is stored in their roots.

"The dandelion is one weed that stores food. The food keeps it alive during the winter. Then in early spring it is ready to bloom. The root grows deep into the ground. That is the reason dandelions are so hard to kill."

"You have to dig up the root to kill a dandelion plant," said Bob. "It's a hard job. I've done it and I know!"

"Here are some pictures of other weeds that store food in their roots," said Mr. Thorne.

Mullein

Burdock

"Let's go outside and look for these weeds," said Jimmy. "Maybe we can find other weeds that store food in their roots."

The How and Why Club adjourned to look for weeds that had stored food in their roots. These are some that they found.

Black-eyed Susan

Wild Carrot

Plantain

A Trip to the Woods

It was a Saturday afternoon in early April. There had been a severe wind storm the night before. Dick's father wanted to see if any damage had been done in the woods on his farm. Dick and Bob wanted to go with him.

The day was perfect for a hike. As the boys walked along with Dick's father, they noticed that the buds on the trees were beginning to turn green. The leaves of wild flowers were pushing up through the ground. The pussy willows were covered with long yellow catkins.

The sky was clear overhead. There were only a few feathery clouds. The sunshine felt good and the air was full of the smell of warm earth.

They walked farther into the woods. The branches of the trees made shadows on the ground. The buds on some of the trees were opening and looked fuzzy in the sunlight.

Suddenly Bob cried, "Look at that tree. The storm must have blown it over!"

Ahead of them lay a big tree. Its roots were torn out of the ground. Its branches spread high above them.

The boys started toward the tree. "Wait," said Dick's father. "There's something on the branches."

There were dozens of butterflies flying about the branches and twigs of the tree.

"What are they doing?" asked Dick.

"They are probably getting nectar from the flowers," said his father.

"I don't see any flowers. Trees don't have flowers on them," said Bob.

"Oh, yes, they do," said Dick's father. "Don't you see how fuzzy the ends of the twigs look? Look closely. You can see many thread-like stems with tiny yellow balls on the ends. Those stems with their yellow balls are *stamens*. The ends of the stamens have pollen in them. Pollen looks like yellow dust. The part of a stamen which contains pollen is yellow. On this tree the part of the flower where the seeds grow is red."

"But they don't look like flowers," said Bob.

"That is because they don't have petals," said Dick's father. "Flowers like tulips have petals. These flowers don't."

Bob sniffed the air. "The flowers smell good. What kind of tree is it?"

"It's a maple tree," said Dick's father.

"We tapped a maple tree," said Bob, "but it didn't look like this."

"You tapped a hard-maple tree," said Dick's father. "This is a soft maple. That is a hard maple over there. Can you see the difference?"

The boys looked at the two trees. "Well," said Dick, "the bark of the hard maple is darker all the way up than this soft maple. The top of this soft maple is light gray."

"Good observation," said Dick's father.

"The bark of the hard maple looks rougher," said Bob.

"The tree looks as if it had grown too big for its skin," laughed Dick.

"It does have some big ridges going up and down," said his father.

"The hard maple isn't blooming, is it?" asked Bob.

"No, hard maples bloom later than the soft maples," said Dick's father.

"How did you know that this is a maple tree?" asked Bob.

"There are several ways to tell," said Dick's father. "When you observe trees, you learn to know them. First you observe the shape of the tree. Then you look at its bark. You can also tell trees by their buds, flowers, and leaves. The buds on a maple tree are always opposite each other."

He took a branch from the fallen tree and showed the boys how the buds and twigs grew opposite or right across from each other on the branch.

"This is one thing that helps us to know the maple trees," he went on. "The easiest way to know them is by looking at their leaves."

"When the leaves come out will you come and help our science club find out about the trees in our school yard?" asked Bob.

"I'll be glad to," said Dick's father.

Bob and Dick reported to the How and Why Club the next Monday. They told the other children about the soft-maple tree with its butterfly visitors. The children were anxious to know if there were any soft maples in the school yard. They went to the windows and looked out.

"I think that is one," said Dick, pointing to a tree with light-gray branches and reddish flowers.

"You are right," said Mr Thorne. "That is a silver maple, and a silver maple is one of the soft maples."

"Are there different kinds of soft maples?" asked Nancy.

"Yes," said Mr. Thorne, "and there are different kinds of hard maples, too. It is difficult to tell them apart before the leaves come out."

"My father said that, too," said Dick.

"Could we tap soft-maple trees?" asked Jane.

"We could, but there is so much water in the sap that it takes a long time to boil it down. That's why people usually tap hard-maple trees."

Bob and Dick told about the flowers on the trees. The children decided to watch for other trees to bloom.

"The pussy willows were in bloom, too," said Dick. "They looked like yellow caterpillars. My father says that the gray pussies which come very early in the spring are just buds."

"The willows and poplars bloom very early," said Mr. Thorne. "The bees often gather nectar and pollen from them before other flowers are in bloom."

Several weeks passed. The days grew longer. Spring rains and more hours of sunshine made the buds open fast. By the last of May the trees were covered with leaves. The children began to bring leaves from different trees. They wanted to know the names of the trees.

"I know how we can tell which ones are maple leaves," said Jane. "We can see which ones match the leaves on the maple trees in the school yard."

The children took their leaves and went to the yard. On the hard-maple tree they found a leaf like this.

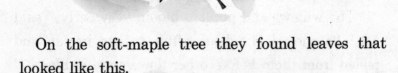

On the soft-maple tree they found leaves that looked like this.

"Each leaf has five points," said Jimmy. "But the soft-maple leaf is more jagged."

"It has fine-toothed edges," said Mr. Thorne. "Some leaves have smooth edges; some have coarse-toothed edges; some have wavy edges."

"I have a soft-maple leaf," said Nancy. "It came from a tree in our yard at home. We must have a soft-maple tree."

Jane and Susan had hard-maple leaves.

Jimmy had a leaf that looked like this.

"It's a horse-chestnut leaf," he explained.

"Oh, yes, we studied about them last year," said Susan. "Is there a horse-chestnut tree in the school yard? Let's look for one."

The children found several trees that they already knew.

Here are pictures of the leaves of the trees. Can you find leaves like them?

American Elm

Poplar

Horse-Chestnut

Oak

The next day Dick's father helped the Club name the trees they didn't know. They learned to know these leaves.

Black Walnut

Beech

These are leaves which Jack has learned to know.
They grow in the mountains in the West.

Aspen

Mountain Maple

Martha Lou and Randy find these leaves in the
South, where they live.

Magnolia

Live Oak

This is a leaf which Rita and Pablo know. This
leaf grows in the desert.

Mesquite

Some Drummers

Rat-a-tat-tat!

Bob sat up in bed and rubbed his eyes. Where
was the alarm clock? The house was still. No one
else stirred. Bob lay down again. He must have
been dreaming. No, there it was again and again.
Bob listened. No sound came from the other bed-
rooms. Where could that alarm clock be?

Bob buried his head in the pillow so he couldn't
hear the sound.

Later at breakfast Bob asked who had set the
alarm clock to ring so early. Mother and Dad
looked surprised.

"The alarm clock didn't ring this morning," said
Mother.

"I heard it several times," said Bob. "It went
like this—*rat-a-tat-tat.*"

Dad laughed. "I think I know what your alarm clock was," he said. "Probably it will ring again tomorrow morning. I'll listen for it."

Dad wouldn't tell Bob more about it. "Wait and see," he said.

The next morning Bob was awake when the sound began again. Dad came into his room.

"Come to the window and look up at the roof," he said. Bob looked. There on the tin ridge was a bird. His head went back and forth so fast to the tin that it did sound like an alarm clock. *Rat-a-tat-tat! Rat-a-tat-tat!* his beak went against the tin.

"A woodpecker!" cried Bob. "What makes him drum on the tin?"

"I don't know exactly," said Dad. "But woodpeckers often do that in the spring. Why don't you ask Mr. Thorne?"

Bob had a good question for the How and Why Club that day. The rest of the children were interested. They had so many questions that they decided to study woodpeckers in the science class. These are some of the things they wanted to know:

1. How can you tell that a bird belongs to the woodpecker family?
2. What are the habits of woodpeckers?
3. Why do woodpeckers sometimes drum on tin?
4. Do woodpeckers harm trees?

"How can we find the answers to the questions?" asked Susan.

"We can look for woodpeckers. We can see whether they are all alike," suggested Jane.

"We can watch them and tell each other what we see," said Jimmy.

"Last year a pair of woodpeckers had a nest in our yard," said Bob. "Perhaps they will nest there again this year and we can watch them."

"Those are good suggestions," said Mr. Thorne. "Would you like to go outdoors now and see something I found yesterday?"

Mr. Thorne led them to a maple tree and stopped. At first no one saw anything unusual. Then Bob spied some holes in the tree trunk. The holes were almost square. They were in rows on the tree. The holes were filled with sap. The children were excited. They wondered why the holes were in such even rows. Mr. Thorne told the children that he had seen the holes being made. "You may see, too, if you wait quietly," he said.

Suddenly a bird darted to the trunk of a nearby tree. It clung there a minute looking toward the children. They were so still that the bird didn't seem afraid. He flew to the trunk above their heads. Each child held his breath with excitement. The bird was drinking the sap that had collected in the little wells in the bark. His brush-like tongue reached into one hole after another to get the sweet sap. He clung to the tree trunk with his sharp claws and braced himself with his stiff tail feathers. The children could see his red bib with its black border.

The bird finished getting the sap that had collected and flew to another tree.

"Was that a woodpecker?" asked Nancy. "He looked like one but he didn't peck the tree."

"Watch him now," suggested Mr. Thorne.

This time the bird *was* pecking. He worked away, chiseling out the same kind of holes that were in the first tree. Finally he flew away as he had done before.

"He'll come back after sap has collected in the holes," said Mr. Thorne. "This kind of woodpecker feeds on sap in early spring."

"He taps the trees for sap just as we tapped the maple tree, doesn't he?" laughed Susan. "What's his name?"

"This woodpecker is called a *sapsucker*," said Mr. Thorne. "There are several kinds of sapsuckers. This one is called a yellow-bellied sapsucker."

"Doesn't it hurt the trees to have all those holes in them?" asked Jane.

"It would if the birds made enough holes all the way around them. The trees might die," said Mr. Thorne. "Sapsuckers eat nothing but sap early in the spring. Later they eat insects just as other woodpeckers do."

"I always thought woodpeckers bored holes in trees," said Bob when they were back in their room. "The sapsucker just hit the tree with his beak."

"Yes," answered Mr. Thorne. "A woodpecker's beak is something like a chisel. Did you ever see a carpenter hammer a chisel against wood? That is the way a woodpecker makes a hole."

"But not all woodpeckers eat sap, do they?" asked Jimmy.

"No, only the sapsuckers. The chief food of woodpeckers is insects. There are many insect larvae under the bark of trees. A woodpecker makes a hole above the larva. Then it spears the larva with its long tongue. Most woodpeckers have hard-pointed tips on their tongues. The end of a sapsucker's tongue is like a brush."

Mr. Thorne drew some pictures on the board.

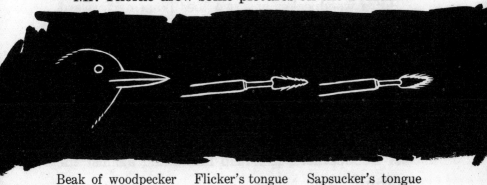

Beak of woodpecker   Flicker's tongue   Sapsucker's tongue

"Then that is one way we can tell birds that belong to the woodpecker family. We can tell them by their beaks and the way they use their tongues," said Bob.

"We can tell them by looking at their tail feathers," Jane said. "Their tail feathers are stiff and pointed."

"Good," said Mr. Thorne. "The third way to know them is by their feet. A robin's foot has three toes pointing forward and one pointing backward like this.

"But a woodpecker has two toes pointing forward and two pointing backward like this."

"A woodpecker's feet help him stand against the tree trunk," said Nancy.

"Let's make lists of all the woodpeckers we see,"
said Jimmy. "Let's start our lists with the yellow-
bellied sapsucker."

Other woodpeckers the children saw were the
flicker, the downy woodpecker, the red-headed
woodpecker, and the hairy woodpecker.

A Pair of Flickers

"Mr. Thorne, may we go to my yard today?" asked Bob one morning when he came to school.

"Why, Bob? Do you have something to show us?"

"A flicker is building a nest. It's fun to watch it."

Mr. Thorne was glad to go with the How and Why Club. Soon the children came to a tree in Bob's yard. The ground under the tree was sprinkled with bits of wood that looked like tiny chips. Suddenly there was a shower of more bits of wood. The children looked up in time to see a flicker's head at a hole. Then it disappeared. They could hear tapping in the dead branch where the bird was working. Then its head came out of the hole. Its beak was full of more bits of wood. The chips came down in a shower.

"Why! She blew them!" exclaimed Nancy.

The children laughed. It was funny.

"The female is working," said Bob.

"How do you know it's the female?" asked Jimmy.

"She doesn't have a mustache," said Bob.

"A mustache!" cried Jane. "Who ever heard of a bird with a mustache!"

"The male flicker has black marks back of his beak. They look like a mustache," said Bob. "I've been watching these flickers ever since that first day when one woke me up. I didn't know what kind of woodpecker it was then."

The bird's head appeared again with its beak full of chips.

"If Bob has been watching these birds, perhaps he can tell us more about them," suggested Mr. Thorne.

"Well," said Bob. "I read a bird book to find out why the male flicker was drumming on the house. Men who study birds think that male flickers drum to tell other males to stay away. The bird book calls it *choosing territory*. Last year a cardinal chose his territory in our yard. He sang from trees around the territory. He drove other male cardinals away.

"The flicker drummed, then he made a funny noise like *flick-er*, *flick-er*, *flick-er*. That's how flickers got their name. One day I saw two male flickers fighting in the yard. The one that won the fight stayed in the yard.

"The most interesting thing I saw happened when the female flicker came into the yard. The male bird began to notice her. The two birds stood on a branch and made motions at each other with their beaks. They walked toward each other waving their heads back and forth. Then they walked away from each other again. Sometimes the male bird spread his wings and tail so that the yellow lining showed."

"The male bird was courting the female," said Mr. Thorne. "Most birds have interesting courting habits before they mate. Many of them spread their feathers out or fluff them up and strut. Sometimes the female seems to pay attention to the male and sometimes she doesn't. After the birds have mated, they start building nests in which eggs are laid."

Several times, while Bob and Mr. Thorne were talking, the flicker dumped more chips on the ground.

"How deep does she make the nest?" asked Dick.

"She makes it about one and a half feet deep," said Mr. Thorne. "Then she lays her eggs on the chips that are left on the bottom of the hole. Perhaps we can come again after the eggs hatch and see the young birds as they are being fed."

Several weeks later Bob announced that he had seen the male flicker poking his head into the nest hole. He said he could hear young birds and could see beaks coming out of the hole. The club planned to go to the tree.

When the children reached the tree, both parent birds were gone from the nest. Soon the male came back. First the male, then the female, came to the tree. When the bird alighted on the tree, there was a buzzing sound inside the tree. Three heads appeared at the hole and the parent bird rammed its beak down a young one's throat.

"I should think that sharp beak would go right down through the baby's neck!" exclaimed Jimmy. "Why does the parent poke so hard?"

"The young birds can't swallow food unless it touches the back of their tongues. The parent makes sure by poking the food down. When the birds are older, they will spear their own food."

"Well, I wouldn't want to be fed like that," remarked Susan as they left the tree.

Two weeks later Bob reported that the young birds had left the nest. "I saw one of them on the ground with its beak in an ant hill," he said.

"Flickers eat ants," said Mr. Thorne. "They lap up the ants with their tongues. It's much easier than digging in a tree for food."

"Woodpeckers certainly have interesting habits," said Bob. "The sapsucker eats sap in the spring. When the sap stops flowing, the bird eats insects and feeds insects to its young. It flies south in the winter.

"The flicker usually goes south, too. The flicker eats insects.

"The downy woodpecker makes holes in the bark to get its insects. But it stays in the North all winter. In the winter it will eat suet if it can find any. When food is hard to find in winter you should place suet where birds can find it.

"The hairy woodpecker looks much like the downy woodpecker, only it's bigger. Sometimes the hairy woodpecker stays in the North all winter.

"The red-headed woodpecker also gets insects from under bark. But it will eat other things such as bread. It usually flies south in winter."

"All woodpeckers make their nests by digging holes in dead trees or poles. All of them are much alike in the way they care for their young," said Mr. Thorne. "Are woodpeckers helpful or harmful?"

"Woodpeckers are helpful," said Jimmy. "They eat harmful insects. The insects they eat would harm the trees."

"I always thought a woodpecker was just a wood-pecker," said Dick. "I didn't know there were so many kinds."

"That's the way with most families of animals," said Mr. Thorne. "Different kinds belong to the same family. Scientists have put them together in a family because they are alike in some ways. When you know why they belong to the same family, you can recognize them. The kind of beak and feet a bird has usually tells its family."

Randy's Experiment

"May I open the window, Mother?" asked Randy. "Martha Lou and I are getting hot."

"Yes," said Mother. "This room needs ventilation."

"What is ventilation?" asked Martha Lou. "I wish you would tell me about it."

"We have ventilation when air goes out of a room and fresh air comes in," said Randy.

"I know that," said Martha Lou. "But what causes it to happen? What will make the cold air come in and the hot air go out?"

"I will show you an experiment," said Randy. "You sit down while I get some things."

In a few minutes Randy came back with a short stick and some tissue paper. He tore the paper into narrow ribbons and fastened them to one end of the stick. Martha Lou watched closely.

Randy opened the window at the bottom. He opened it just a little. He opened the window a little at the top, too. Then he took the stick and held it near the place where the window was open at the bottom. The paper ribbons blew away from the open window.

Then Randy got onto a chair. He held the stick near the opening at the top of the window. The paper ribbons blew in the opposite direction. They blew into the open space above the window.

"Oh," said Martha Lou. "The air comes in at the bottom of the window. It goes out at the top."

"Our bodies use oxygen and give off carbon dioxide," said Randy. "When we live in a room, we use up much oxygen. We give off much carbon dioxide. Our bodies also give off heat and moisture. So we open a window at the top and at the bottom. Fresh air comes in. The air with carbon dioxide goes out. We call that ventilation. That's why Mother keeps our windows open some of the time."

"Let's fix another stick and both try the experiment," said Martha Lou.

So Randy fixed a stick for Martha Lou. Martha Lou held hers at the bottom of the window. Randy held his at the top.

"See! Air comes in and air goes out at the same time," said Randy.

"Why does it work that way?" asked Martha Lou.

"Stop and think," said Randy. "What happens to air when it gets warm?"

"Warm air expands," said Martha Lou.

"That's right," said Randy. "Warm air expands. It gets lighter. Cold air is heavier than warm air. So when you open the window the heavier, cold air pushes the lighter, warm air out of its way. The cold

air pours into the room. The warm air is forced up."

"But why doesn't cold air pour in at the top of the window, too?" asked Martha Lou.

"A little of it does come in," said Randy. "But the warm air is being pushed out so fast that it is hard for the cold air to come in."

"I see now," said Martha Lou. "Cold air comes in at the bottom. It is heavier so it goes down. It pushes the warm air up and out at the top."

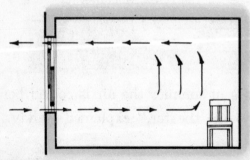

"Sometimes ventilation is done by machines," said Randy.

"Do you mean machines to open and close windows?" asked Martha Lou.

"No," said Randy. "Machines to make the air move. There are no windows in the movie theater in town."

"That's right," said Martha Lou. "How is the theater ventilated?"

"The air is forced into the theater by a big fan," said Randy. "The big fan draws the air in from the outside. It blows the fresh air into the theater. Then the air goes out at the top. Here, I'll draw a diagram for you.

BASEMENT

"Sometimes in summer the air is cooled before it is blown into the theater," explained Randy.

Air is brought into the machine here.

Air is forced into the theater here.

This is a screen with water running on it. It washes all dust and dirt out of the air.

These are coils which contain cold water. They cool the air.

This is the big fan. It forces the clean, cool air into the theater.

"Our class went through the theater with Mr. Jackson. He runs the theater. He explained its ventilation.

"You see, when the machine runs, it brings in fresh air. The air is washed, cooled, and sent into the theater."

"The machine can't work in winter, can it?" asked Martha Lou.

"Yes, it works just as well. Only the coils have warm water in them. In the summer, cold, clean air goes into the theater. In the winter it is warm, clean air."

"That's a good way to ventilate," said Martha Lou.

The Compass

"North, Northeast, East, Southeast, South, Southwest, West, Northwest, North," muttered Ted.

"What are you saying to yourself?" laughed Joyce.

"I'm going to join the Air Scouts soon," said Ted. "I'll have to learn about a compass so that I can tell directions. I'm learning the points of the compass now."

"What do you mean by the 'points' of a compass?" asked Joyce.

"I can explain that to you," said Ted. "Here is the compass the Scout Master let me bring home. It is a dandy one. Around the edge of the compass are the letters N, E, S, and W. They stand for the points North, East, South, and West. That's what I'm learning now."

"I don't see how that helps you find direction,"
said Joyce. "What does that little arrow do?"

"The real name for that arrow is *needle*," said
Ted. "One end of the needle is blue. That end
always points to the north. If I want to find any
direction with the compass, I hold the compass
level or put it on a level surface. Then I turn the
compass until the letter N is right beneath the blue
point of the needle. Then the other directions are
marked in big letters. All flyers use compasses to
help find their way. A compass is an important instrument for an Air Scout to know about."

"It sounds easy," said Joyce. "I still don't understand why the blue end of the needle always points to the north. Are you sure about that?"

"Yes, I'm sure it always points north," answered Ted. "But I don't know why. Suppose we ask Uncle Don if he can explain it to us."

When Ted and Joyce questioned Uncle Don about the needle of the compass, Uncle Don smiled and said, "Ted, open my desk drawer. Bring the two little red boxes that are there."

"Now," said Uncle Don, when Ted had brought the boxes, "I think we can find out how your compass works." He took from the boxes four pieces of metal.

"That's a magnet," said Ted, pointing to the one shaped like a horseshoe. "May I play with it, Uncle Don?"

"Of course you may, Ted," answered Uncle Don. "You will have just as much fun with these others. They are all magnets. The one you have is called a *horseshoe* magnet. This other curved one is a *U-magnet*. These two straight ones are *bar* magnets."

"I didn't know there were different kinds of magnets," said Joyce. "Will they all pick up things?"

"They pull only certain metals," said Uncle Don.

"I know they pull iron and steel," said Ted. "Let's try some other metals."

"You might try a penny," said Uncle Don, putting one on the table.

Ted tried to pick up the penny with his magnet.

"The penny doesn't stick to the magnet," he said.

"You don't mean that," said Uncle Don. "Metals don't stick to magnets, but magnets have power to draw certain metals. We usually say that magnets *attract* certain metals."

"Thanks for correcting me," said Ted. "I'll say it the right way this time. The magnet didn't attract the penny. The penny is made of copper. Magnets don't attract copper."

"Magnets do attract tin, though," said Joyce. "My magnet attracts this tin cup."

"I'll have to correct you this time," said Uncle Don. "Magnets don't attract tin. There is a thin layer of tin on the cup. Under the tin there is iron. The magnet attracts the iron."

"Do magnets draw through other things which they don't attract?" asked Joyce.

"The best way to find out is to try," said Uncle Don. "Just put a piece of paper over these thumb tacks, and then try your magnet."

Joyce picked up the tacks through the paper.

"Will magnets attract through glass, Uncle Don?" asked Ted.

"We can experiment to find out," said Uncle Don. "Here are some iron filings in the box. Sprinkle them on this glass plate. Now put a magnet underneath and see what happens."

Ted put the U-magnet under the plate.

Some of the filings moved immediately. Uncle Don tapped the plate with his finger. The filings moved again until they looked like this.

"Oh, boy!" said Ted. "Magnets attract through glass. And see how the filings are arranged around each end of the magnet."

"The filings are drawn to the ends of the magnet. The ends are called *poles*," said Uncle Don. "This one marked N is the north pole of the magnet; this one marked S is the south pole of the magnet."

"Why are they called north and south poles?" asked Ted. "The earth has a North and a South Pole, but I didn't know magnets have them, too."

To explain this, Uncle Don hung a bar magnet from a wooden frame. He hung it with silk thread.

The magnet swung around several times. Then it stopped.

"In what direction is the N pole pointing?" asked Uncle Don.

Ted looked at his compass. "The N pole is pointing north," he said. "That's why it is called the north pole. The other end points south so it is the south pole."

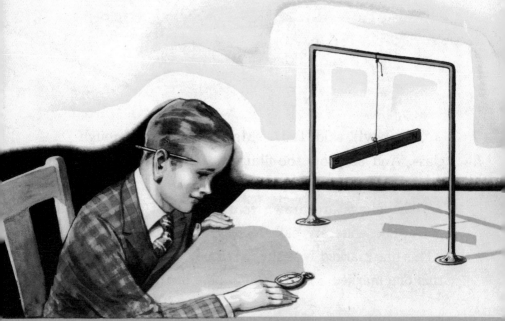

"I wonder what would happen if we held two magnets together," said Joyce. She held the S pole of one bar magnet near the S pole of the magnet that was hung on the silk thread. Immediately the hanging magnet moved away from the one that Joyce held.

"See what happened," she said. "Magnets don't attract magnets."

"That's strange," said Ted. "Let me try it."

Ted held the N pole near the S pole of the hanging magnet. Immediately the ends were attracted to each other. They snapped together.

Ted was as surprised as Joyce to see the magnets come together. Then he said, "The N pole of one magnet attracted the S pole of the other magnet. The S pole did not attract another S pole. They pushed away from each other."

"You observed that well," said Uncle Don. "We call the N pole of one magnet and the S pole of another magnet *unlike* poles. Unlike poles attract each other.

"Two N poles are *like* poles. So are two S poles. Like poles push away from each other. We say that like poles *repel* each other."

"Do horseshoe magnets have north and south poles, too?" asked Joyce. "This horseshoe magnet isn't marked like the bar magnets."

"Horseshoe magnets have north and south poles," answered Uncle Don. "If they aren't marked, we can easily find out which is north and which is south."

"I know how to test them," said Ted.

He touched the N pole of the bar magnet to one end of the horseshoe magnet. The poles did not attract each other. "That's the N pole of the horseshoe magnet," said Ted. "I put both N poles together. Like poles do not attract each other."

"Why do you have magnets in your desk, Uncle Don?" asked Joyce.

"Sometimes I use them to make my tools into magnets. I can pick up little screws on the end of a screw driver that has been made into a magnet. When we make tools into magnets, we *magnetize* them."

"May we magnetize something?" asked Joyce.

"Yes, indeed," said Uncle Don. "How would you like to magnetize a screw driver? You may magnetize a needle, too."

Ted magnetized a screw driver. He rubbed the screw driver with one end of the magnet. He rubbed the magnet along the screw driver in one direction. He did this several times; then he picked up thumb tacks with the screw driver.

Joyce rubbed a needle with a magnet. When she had finished, Uncle Don said, "Let's float your needle in a dish of water."

"A needle won't float," laughed Ted.

"We can try, anyway," said Uncle Don. He put a flat cork in a dish of water. Carefully he placed the needle on the cork. When Uncle Don took his hand away, the cork with the needle on it floated. It turned around slowly and then stopped.

"The needle turns in the same direction as the bar magnet turned," said Joyce.

"So it does," said Ted. "The needle is pointing north. It works like the compass needle."

Uncle Don smiled.

"You're a good teacher, Uncle Don," said Ted. "You taught us about magnets. Then you let us find out that a compass is really a magnetized needle."

How Electricity Works

One evening Ted and Joyce and Uncle Don went to a band concert in the park. While they were there, a storm came up. They heard thunder. Then they saw flashes of lightning zigzagging across the sky. Suddenly the rain came and everybody ran for shelter.

Uncle Don and the children ran home.

"We should have stood under a tree in the park till the worst of the storm was over," suggested Joyce as she looked at her wet dress.

"Under a tree is a poor place to stand during a storm," said Uncle Don. "Trees often attract lightning. If you were standing under a tree when a flash of lightning struck, you might be hurt."

"Whew!" said Ted. "Let's keep away from trees during thunderstorms after this, Joyce."

When Ted returned from changing his clothes, he said, "Uncle Don, why is lightning so dangerous?"

"Lightning is really a great big spark of electricity," answered Uncle Don. "The electricity collects on the drops of water in the clouds. When two clouds which contain electricity come close together, the electricity jumps across the space and makes the spark which we call lightning."

"I can make sparks myself," said Joyce. "Sometimes when I rub my feet on the carpet and then touch a radiator or a door knob, a little spark jumps from my fingers."

"I've made sparks like that by stroking cats or dogs," said Ted.

"Those sparks are electricity, too," said Uncle Don. "They are the same kind of electricity that lightning is. You can make electricity like that by rubbing some materials together. Rub this fountain pen on my sleeve and then hold it near the papers on my desk."

Joyce rubbed Uncle Don's fountain pen on his coat sleeve several times. She held the pen near the paper. "It pulls the paper," she said.

"You generated electricity by rubbing the pen on the wool cloth. Because of electricity, the paper sticks to the pen," said Uncle Don.

"You can do the same thing with a glass rod or with a hard rubber comb. If you rub them with silk or wool, you can generate electricity."

"Could Mother run her electric sweeper with this electricity?" asked Joyce.

"I'm afraid not," answered Uncle Don. "You can generate only a little electricity by rubbing things together. The electricity that you generate here isn't useful. It cannot be used to run the motor in an electric sweeper. It will not make an iron hot. You cannot generate enough to make it flow from one place to another. To be useful, electricity must flow from the power plant where it is generated to the places where it will be used."

"What do you mean by 'flow,' Uncle Don?" asked Ted. "I thought only liquids would flow."

"Liquids do flow," said Uncle Don. "We also say that electricity flows along wires from one place to another. Sometimes electricity is stored. Here, for instance, is a dry cell. Useful electricity is stored in it."

From a desk drawer Uncle Don took a dry cell, an electric bell, and some fine copper wire.

"Can you connect the dry cell and the bell so that the bell will ring?" Uncle Don asked.

Ted cut two pieces of wire. He attached them to the two screws or *terminals* on the top of the dry cell and to the two screws on the bell. The bell began to ring.

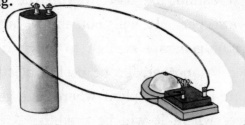

When he took the end of one wire from the bell, the bell stopped ringing.

"Why don't you connect both wires to one screw on the bell?" asked Joyce. Ted connected both wires as Joyce suggested. The bell did not ring.

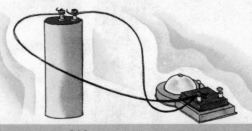

"The bell didn't ring because the current didn't flow through the bell. The electric current has to make a complete circle like this. The path that the electricity travels over is called a *circuit*."

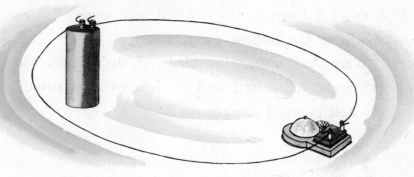

"I understand now that the electricity flows from one terminal of the dry cell through the bell, and back to the other terminal," said Ted. "But when somebody rings our doorbell, he just pushes a button. How does the button work, Uncle Don?"

"We use a *switch* to turn our electric current on and off," said Uncle Don. "Then we don't have to touch the wire itself. We can use a switch with the dry cell, too. We can see how it works. There are many types of switches. A *knife* switch is the simplest type. It opens and closes like a knife. The blade is made of copper. Let's use it to ring the bell."

Ted connected the wires through the switch. He connected them to the dry cell and to the bell as shown in the picture.

When he lowered the blade of the switch, the bell rang. When he raised the blade of the switch, the bell stopped ringing.

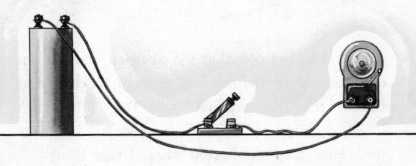

"I see that, now," said Joyce. "The blade of the switch is made of copper just as the wire is. The current flows through the switch when the blade is down. When the blade is up, the current stops. The switch acts like a broken wire."

"Exactly," said Uncle Don. "The switch has a handle made of rubber or wood. Electricity will

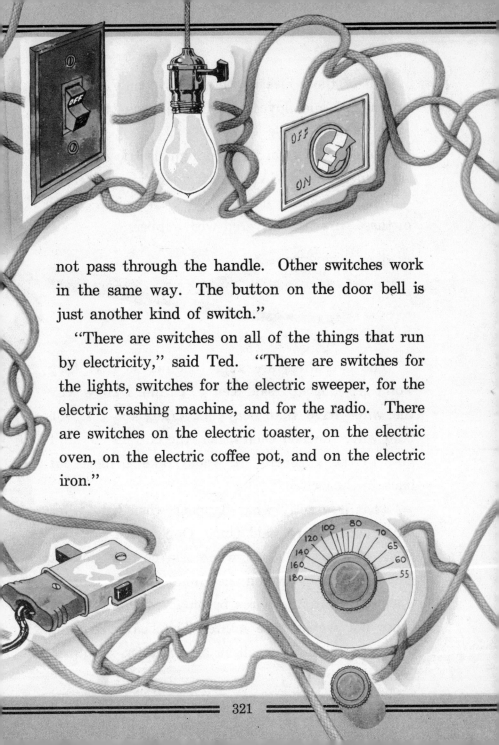

not pass through the handle. Other switches work
in the same way. The button on the door bell is
just another kind of switch."

"There are switches on all of the things that run
by electricity," said Ted. "There are switches for
the lights, switches for the electric sweeper, for the
electric washing machine, and for the radio. There
are switches on the electric toaster, on the electric
oven, on the electric coffee pot, and on the electric
iron."

"All of those electric things have only one wire on them," said Joyce. "This bell has two wires. Why is that, Uncle Don?"

"Here is a piece of wire from an electric sweeper," said Uncle Don. "Let's cut it apart."

Inside the heavy covering were two wires. Each of these wires was covered with rubber.

"The two wires are kept together so that they won't get tangled," said Ted. "I think I know why the wires have that heavy covering, too. If the bare wires touched each other, the current couldn't flow to the sweeper. It would take a short cut back to the switch."

"That is exactly what happens when bare wires touch each other," said Uncle Don. "We say that there is a *short circuit* when the current doesn't flow all the way around the circuit. When there is a short circuit, the wires become very hot. Sometimes hot wires cause a fire. The heavy covering is a protection. We call it an *insulator*. Rubber, dry wood, and glass are good insulators because electricity does not flow through them."

"Oh, then electricity doesn't flow through everything," said Joyce.

"No, it doesn't," said Uncle Don. "Some things won't carry a current at all. Wood and rubber will not carry a current. Copper carries a current very well. Iron and lead wires carry electricity, too, but the electricity has to work so hard when it flows through iron wires that the wires get hot. Metals that do not carry electricity easily are used to get heat."

"That explains the electric toaster and the electric oven," said Ted. "The wires in the oven and in the toaster are metals like that. When the current flows through them, they become hot enough to cook food or to toast bread. They get 'red' hot."

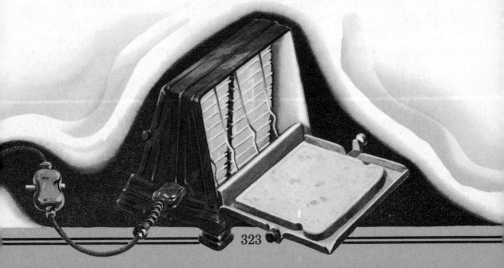

"You said that lead also gets hot when current flows over it," said Joyce. "Are lead wires used in toasters and electric irons, too?"

"No," said Uncle Don. "Lead is very soft. When it becomes hot, it melts. Lead is used in *fuses*."

"I know what fuses are," said Ted. "There are two of them in that box on the wall."

"That's right," said Uncle Don. "Here are some old fuses that have burned out. Can you see the difference between good ones and these old ones?"

"Oh, yes," said Joyce. "The wire inside an old one is broken. The fuse looks black."

"The wire is made of lead," said Uncle Don. "The lead in the old fuses got too hot and melted."

"A short circuit must have caused the lead to melt," said Ted. "When the fuses burned out, the circuit was broken. A fuse is something like a switch. It breaks the circuit when something is wrong."

"It prevents wires from getting too hot and starting fires," said Uncle Don.

Storms

The next day Ted and Joyce were discussing the storm. "It was interesting to learn about electricity," said Joyce, "but I wonder what made the storm come so fast."

"Yes," said Ted. "When we went to the concert the sky was clear. All of a sudden it began to rain."

"It wasn't quite that sudden," said Uncle Don. "I noticed the cloud coming up before we heard the thunder. I wasn't surprised. We often have a thunderstorm at the end of a hot day."

"Why is that?" asked Joyce.

"Well," said Uncle Don, "you know that heat makes water evaporate. During the day the sun is hot. It heats the ground, rivers, and lakes. Water evaporates rapidly and is carried up by air currents. As it goes higher and higher the air is cooled. Do you remember what happens to evaporated water when it cools?"

"It comes out of the air and makes a cloud," said Ted.

"That's right," said Uncle Don.

"Yesterday was very hot. The air was full of moisture. As long as the sun was up, the air was quite warm. The water was in the air but you couldn't see it. In the evening when the sun set, the air became cooler. The water came out of the air and formed a cloud. So much water formed in the cloud that the air couldn't hold it up. It came down as rain."

"Sometimes there is hail in the summer," said Joyce. "What makes hail?"

"If rain starts to fall and the wind carries the raindrops up into freezing air, the drops freeze. The little drops of ice start down again. The wind catches them and up they go into a cloud. They get a layer of water. As they're tossed higher the water freezes. The more times they go up and down, the more layers of ice the drops get. When they finally fall, we have hail."

"I remember when we had a hailstorm last June," said Ted. "The clouds looked green. You said there was wind in them."

"Yes," said Uncle Don. "Do you remember the layers in the hailstones we cut? Those were large hailstones."

"Rain, hail, snow, and sleet are all caused by changes in temperature," Uncle Don went on. "When the temperature of the air is above freezing, the water forms drops. When the temperature of the air is below freezing, crystals are formed."

"Oh, I know," cried Joyce. "Snow is made of crystals."

"So is frost," said Ted.

"Yes," said Uncle Don. "The different kinds of weather are caused by water, air, and changing temperature."

A Vegetable Garden

Pablo wanted a new bicycle. His father suggested that he raise some vegetables to sell. Rita said that she would help Pablo.

Their father gave Pablo and Rita some money to buy seeds. They bought the seeds at a seed store.

When they were home, the children put the seeds into two piles. "We'll plant these seeds out of doors," said Rita. She had packages of these seeds.

Beans	Carrots	Lettuce
Peas	Radishes	Turnips

"We will plant the other seeds in a box," said Pablo. "They must start to grow in the house. We will put them outside after they are good and strong. Father calls that *transplanting*. Father says plants need very good care while they are young. We will plant these seeds in the house and transplant them later."

In his pile he had packages of these seeds:

Cabbages

Tomatoes

Eggplants

Pablo found three boxes that were the right size to use for planting his seeds. Each one was

about three inches deep, thirty inches long, and twenty inches wide.

Pablo and Rita sifted some good rich loam until it was fine. They put it into the boxes.

Pablo read aloud the directions on the cabbage seed package. "Plant the seeds in the ground to a depth of about four times their size through the middle." Pablo had a puzzled look on his face. "What does that mean?"

"You'll have to measure a cabbage seed," said Rita, "then multiply it by four. But I know an easier way. Put four cabbage seeds together. Then measure. You can plant the seeds that deep."

Pablo did this. "I can't plant the seeds very deep," he said. "They are so small that four seeds in a row do not measure very much."

Pablo planted the seeds in rows in one box. The rows were close together. So were the seeds. The seeds were less than one-half inch deep in the soil. He sifted some fine loam on top of the seeds. Then he packed down the soil.

"Now it's time for the water," said Rita. "Let me put it on." She sprinkled water on the soil. She was careful not to make the soil too wet.

The tomato seeds were planted just a little deeper than the cabbage seeds.

The eggplant seeds were planted deeper than the tomato seeds.

The children put the boxes in the sunshine. Every day they put water on the soil. Soon little plants began to grow. The plants grew so fast that soon they were three inches high.

"Now is the time to transplant them," said Pablo. "Father, will you show me how to do it so that I won't lose a single plant?"

"You must find some other large boxes and fill them with loam. Fill them just as you did the first boxes," said Father. "We'll work with a trowel. A trowel is a handy tool to have."

First, he pressed the trowel into the soft soil in the box of cabbage plants. He lifted out a small bunch of plants and soil.

He picked out just one little plant from the bunch. He was careful to keep a little soil around the root of the tiny plant. "Now, I'll transplant it," he said.

He made a little hole in the fresh soil in the box that Pablo had just filled.

He put some water in the hole. He put the little plant into the hole. Then he carefully put a thin stick into the soil near the hole.

He pressed the stick toward the plant. The stick moved the soil toward the plant.

"You see," said Father. "I do not harm the roots of the plant in this way." He pressed the soil tightly around the plant. "There! The plant is set. It should grow very well now. You can transplant the others."

What a lot of plants Rita and Pablo had when they had finished their work! They had boxes and boxes of small plants. The little plants grew. Only a few of them died. In two weeks, the plants were large enough to be put out of doors.

Now Rita and Pablo had to fix their garden plot. They spaded the ground. They raked out the pebbles that were in the soil. They worked the soil until it was soft and fine. They marked the garden plot into rows. The rows were 18 inches apart. They followed a string to make the rows straight.

One day after school, they transplanted their plants to the garden. They used a trowel to take out each plant. They left as much soil as possible around the roots. They put the plant into a hole that had water in it. They pressed the soil around each plant. They put a paper cover over each plant.

"That will keep the sun from wilting the little plants," said Father. "In a day or two you can uncover them."

"I hope we don't lose any of our plants," said Pablo when he was through. "It's a job to transplant. But it's a lot of fun, too. Just think of all the vegetables we'll have to sell."

The next day they planted Rita's seeds.

"The weeds grow as fast as the plants," said Pablo. "I'll have to pull them out."

No sooner had Pablo taken out all the weeds than he had to dig between the rows. He said that he was *cultivating* the plants. Cultivating made the soil softer.

One day Rita called to Pablo, "Oh! the leaves are gone from two tomato plants!"

"Maybe they need water," said Pablo.

"No, the soil isn't dry," said Rita. "See if you can find out what is the matter."

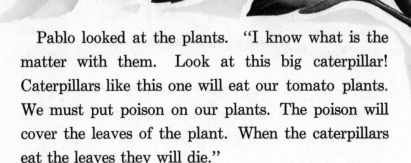

Pablo looked at the plants. "I know what is the matter with them. Look at this big caterpillar! Caterpillars like this one will eat our tomato plants. We must put poison on our plants. The poison will cover the leaves of the plant. When the caterpillars eat the leaves they will die."

Here was some more work for the children. They put poison on the plants. The poison killed the caterpillars that were eating the tender plants. The poison did not kill or harm the plants.

Very soon the radishes and lettuce were ready to sell at a market in town. Pablo put the first money that they earned into a bank.

The beans, peas, carrots, and turnips were soon ready to sell, too, but the plants they had transplanted were slower in growing.

"Do you think the plants will ever have tomatoes and cabbages and eggplants on them?" asked Pablo.

"Oh, yes!" Father laughed. "Just wait. One day you will be saying, 'What can we do with all these tomatoes?'"

At last a tomato plant bloomed. Small green tomatoes grew where the blooms had been. They grew larger and larger. Finally they turned red. When they were a deep rich red, Pablo picked them. He and Rita took them to town and sold them. Every day after that they picked tomatoes.

The eggplants grew, too. At first they were small and pale green. They grew larger and turned to a deep shining purple.

"Aren't they beautiful!" exclaimed Rita. "I'm so glad we raised eggplants. An eggplant is such a pretty vegetable."

Soon they had cabbages, too. The heads were solid. Pablo sold every one that grew.

By fall Rita and Pablo had so many vegetables they could hardly take care of them. Their bank grew heavy with money. One day when Pablo put in a quarter, his bank burst wide open!

"One dollar. Two dollars. Five dollars," counted Pablo. "Oh! we have seventeen dollars and fifty-three cents! That's a lot of money, but not enough to buy the bicycle I want." For a moment Pablo and Rita were disappointed.

"You have worked so hard in your garden, and have been so successful," said Father as he came into the room, "that I will give you the rest of the money you need."

How the children's eyes shone! "Oh, thank you, Father! We have more than half enough in our bank."

Father gave the children some money. That very afternoon they bought their bicycle.

Classes of Animals

Animals that are much alike are put together in a class. We may understand why animals are put in classes if we know more about them. There are several classes of animals.

Mammals

One class of animals is called *Mammals*.

All mammals are put in the same class because:

1. They feed their young milk.
2. They have hair on their skin.
3. They breathe through lungs.
4. They have the same temperature the year around unless they are sick. Animals like these are said to be *warm-blooded*.
5. Their young are born alive.

Mammals may be put together according to the kind of teeth they have.

Dogs and cats are something alike because they have tearing teeth.

These mammals are something alike because they have gnawing teeth: woodchucks, rabbits, squirrels, mice, beavers, prairie dogs, and chipmunks. These animals are called *rodents*.

These mammals are something alike because they chew their cuds: sheep, cows, deer, and goats.

Birds

Another class of animals is called *Birds*.
All birds are put in the same class because:

1. They have feathers.

2. They have wings.

3. They have no teeth.
4. They have beaks instead of lips.

5. They have light-weight bones.
6. They are warm-blooded animals.
7. Their young hatch from eggs.

Reptiles

Another class is called *Reptiles*.

All reptiles are put in the same class because:

1. They have scaly skins.
2. They have very short legs or none at all.
3. They have claws if they have feet.
4. They have tails.
5. Their temperature changes. In winter it isn't so high as it is in summer. Animals like these are called *cold-blooded*.

Amphibians

Another class is called *Amphibians*.

All amphibians are put in the same class because:

1. They have smooth, thin skins.
2. They have no claws on their feet.
3. They have no necks.

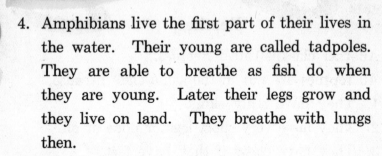

4. Amphibians live the first part of their lives in the water. Their young are called tadpoles. They are able to breathe as fish do when they are young. Later their legs grow and they live on land. They breathe with lungs then.
5. They are cold-blooded animals.
6. Their young hatch from eggs but do not look like their parents.

Fish

Another class is called *Fish*.

All fish are put in the same class because:

1. Most of them have scales on their skin.
2. They have fins instead of legs.
3. They live in water.
4. They are able to breathe in water. They breathe through gills.
5. They are cold-blooded animals.

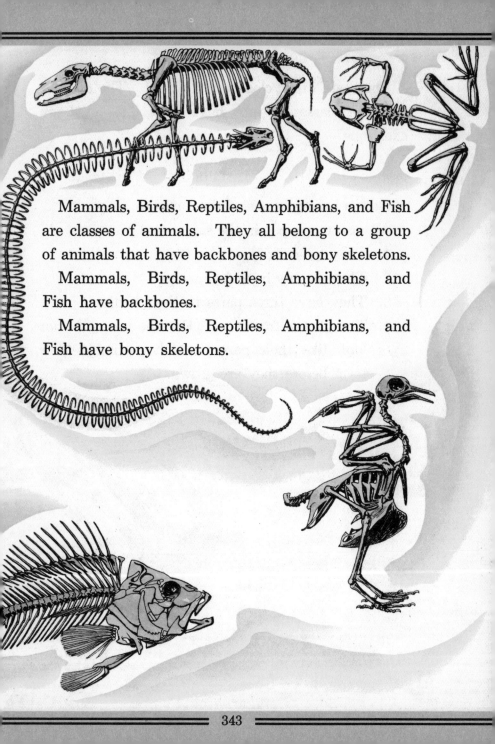

Mammals, Birds, Reptiles, Amphibians, and Fish are classes of animals. They all belong to a group of animals that have backbones and bony skeletons.

Mammals, Birds, Reptiles, Amphibians, and Fish have backbones.

Mammals, Birds, Reptiles, Amphibians, and Fish have bony skeletons.

There are other classes of animals. The animals in these classes do not have backbones or bony skeletons.

Insects

Insects belong in one of these classes.

All insects are put in the same class because:

1. They have six legs.
2. They usually have four wings.
3. They have three parts to their bodies.
4. They hatch from eggs. But the young do not look like their parents. They change their form before they are grown.

Spiders

Spiders belong to another class.

Spiders are put in a class because:

1. They have eight legs.
2. They have no wings.
3. They have two parts to their bodies.
4. Their young hatch from eggs and look like their parents.

Crayfish

Crayfish belong to another class.

Crayfish are put in a class because:

1. They have more than eight legs.
2. They have no wings.
3. They live in water and breathe through gills.
4. Their eggs hatch into little crayfish. The little ones look like their parents.
5. They have a hard crust-like skin.

Can you name the animals on pages 346 and 347?
Can you tell in which class each one belongs?

Some animals are helpful. They should be protected. Birds are helpful. Toads, frogs, salamanders, lizards, and most snakes are helpful. Most spiders are helpful.

Some insects are harmful. They should be killed.

The members of the How and Why Club decided never to kill an animal unless they found it to be harmful. The best way to find out if an animal is harmful is to ask the advice of a scientist.

the End

INDEX

Potatoes, 21; 24–27; 30; 32–33; 35; 116
Prism, 251–252
Protection: of animals, 50; 87; 162; by color, 76; 85
Protein, 124–125; 127

Rabbits, 61–62; 189–190; 339
Rainbow, 250–252
Reflected light, 216; 247–251
Reptiles, 341; 343
Rivers, 73; 233–235; 245
Rocks, 83; 162; 226–227; 229–234
Rodents, 61–62; 65; 67
Roots, 25; 33–34; 51; 61; 68; 70; 96; 264–265; 267; 269; 332

Saliva, 132; 135
Salt, 31; 38; 40; 71
Sap, 255–259; 277; 285–286
Scientists, 17; 31; 37; 125; 159; 173; 180–181; 223; 297; 348
Seeds, 25; 254–255; 264; 328–331
Shadow, 216–217; 220–222
Sheep, 66; 144; 339
Skeleton, 110–112; 147; 151; 343–344
Skin, 138; 152; 338; 341–342; 345
Skulls, 59–61
Soil, 96; 104–105; 227; 229–235; 329–334
Spiders, 73–88; 345; 348; Black Widow, 80: Crab, 84–85; Golden Garden, 81; Jumping, 85–86; Orb Weaver, 80; Tarantula, 87; Trap Door, 86–87

Spoiled food, 164–184
Spores, 169
Squirrels, 61; 63–65; 339
Stamens, 273
Stars, 192–209
Starch, 28; 30–34; 36; 38; 43; 51; 101; 116–127; 132–135; 254–256; 268–269
Stems, 26; 32; 34; 51; 61; 263; 267; 273
Stomach, 136
Storms, 271; 315; 325–327
Sun, 36; 205–209; 211–223; 230; 245–248; 326
Sugar, 28; 32; 36; 43; 116; 123; 127; 132–135; 254–268
Sugar beets, 34; 260–261; 264–268
Sugar cane, 89; 260–263; 268
Sweat, 138

Teeth: beavers', 46; 59–60; 339; canine, 62; 67–71; 339; cavities in, 70; cows', 66; 339; fossils', 158–159; human, 65; 68–71; 108; muskrats', 59; rabbits', 61–62; 339; rodents', 65; 67; 339; sheep's, 66; 339; squirrels', 61; 65; 339
Temperature, 22; 327; 338; 341
Tools, 237–244; 313
Tracks, 146–147; 149; 187–190; 331
Transplanting, 328; 331–333
Trees, 26; 44–48; 51–54; 107; 255–259; 267–268; 315; 271–280; 284; 287